CREATING COFFEE TABLES

An Artistic Approach

CRAIG VANDALL STEVENS

PHOTOGRAPHY BY
BRUCE WATERS

Schiffer Publishing Ltd ®

4880 Lower Valley Road, Atglen, PA 19310 USA

DEDICATION

This book is dedicated to my good friend and teacher, Michael Burns, whose impeccable craftsmanship, patience, and sense of humor are an everlasting inspiration to me.

A Word About Safety

Woodworking is inherently dangerous. Safety equipment greatly reduces the chance of injury in the workshop, as does caution and common sense. If a procedure feels awkward or dangerous, find a safe alternative. Your safety is your own responsibility.

Copyright © 1998 by Craig Vandall Stevens
Library of Congress Catalog Card Number: 98-85759

All rights reserved. No part of this work may be reproduced or used in any form or by any means—graphic, electronic, or mechanical, including photocopying or information storage and retrieval systems—without written permission from the copyright holder.
"Schiffer," "Schiffer Publishing Ltd. & Design," and the "Design of pen and ink well" are registered trademarks of Schiffer Publishing, Ltd.

Designed by Blair Loughrey
Typeset in Korinna / Bernhard Modern BT

ISBN: 0-7643-0623-5
Printed in China

Published by Schiffer Publishing Ltd.
4880 Lower Valley Road
Atglen, PA 19310
Phone: (610) 593-1777; Fax: (610) 593-2002
e-mail: schifferbk@aol.com
Please write for a free catalog.
This book may be purchased from the publisher.
Please include $3.95 for shipping.

In Europe, Schiffer books are distributed by
Bushwood Books
6 Marksbury Avenue
Kew Gardens
Surrey TW9 4JF England
Phone: 44 (0)181 392-8585; Fax: 44 (0)181 392-9876
e-mail: bushwd@aol.com

Please try your bookstore first.

We are interested in hearing from authors with book ideas on related subjects.

CONTENTS

ACKNOWLEDGMENTS

I would like to express my appreciation of Caroline, my wife, for her inspiration and very special support of my work, as well as her sneak-up-from-behind editing style and commentary (the laughing is OK, it's the pointing that bothers me). Also great thanks to my family and friends who express endless interest and support. Special thanks to Terre Meadows for all her help.

Also a note of gratitude to my talented friends and fellow College of the Redwoods graduates Greg "Barney" Smith, Thea Gray, and Mike Prendergast, for their help in keeping me stocked with a fine collection of the narra, kwila, and other ecologically harvested lumber.

Finally I would like to thank the nice folks at Schiffer Publishing for taking an interest in my work, in particular Bruce Waters, my photographer for the project, and Doug Congdon-Martin, for their special skills.

INTRODUCTION

A beautiful coffee table has been part of a long list of furniture pieces my wife, Caroline, and I have wanted in our home for some time. However, like the cobbler, pieces for ourselves often get put off while I work to complete commissioned furniture. We had grown accustomed to a maple, butcher block slab placed on a wicker chest that served the purpose, but which never seemed appropriate for someone who has the good fortune to design and build furniture for a living.

A coffee table is an important focal point in many people's homes. It can serve to display pieces of art, collections of magazines, books, and remote controls, and become an impromptu dining table. Coffee tables can take on a wide variety of styles ranging from very ornate period pieces to contemporary art tables.

One of the most rewarding parts of woodworking and furniture making is being able to design and work on a wide variety of furniture pieces. Different types of furniture require different levels of focus and discipline and require varying degrees of commitment, both in time and in challenge. Designing and making a coffee table represents a unique project for the craftsperson. It offers the reward and satisfaction of completing a beautiful piece of furniture without being so overwhelming that it becomes discouraging. A coffee table project requires forethought and planning. It also helps to develop confident handskills and the attitude to do one's best, especially for someone just beginning to explore furniture making.

In this book I will discuss designing and sketching a coffee table, making a full size mock-up of the project to better visualize its proportions, and the selection of wood. Also laying out, cutting, and milling lumber, joinery, assembling the table, and applying a finish. I'll also discuss the sharpening of cutting tools as well as the benefits of some fine woodworking tools, shop made jigs, and machines.

I hope that in a small way, this book helps to convey a commitment to craftsmanship and the simple enjoyment of making an object.

WOOD

One of the most interesting stages of building a piece of furniture is sorting through stacks of lumber in search of perfect boards—not perfect in the sense that the grain be absolutely straight and generic, although sometimes that is very important, but perfect in the sense of a wood's uniqueness. Perhaps there's a rhythm or sense of movement that an unusual grain graphic gives a plank. The wood may have a place in history or a great story behind it, like English elm's use as the piles that supported London bridge. The species may be unique because it is not usually associated with fine furniture, like hornbeam or honey lo-

cust, or sometimes the wood is perfect because it fulfills the type of woodworking experience you'd like to have on the project.

There's something appealing about the possibility that somewhere in a stack of hardwoods is a plank that will stir an idea and give it energy, allowing the idea to begin taking shape in the mind's eye. Or a sketch I've been working on can come into clear focus upon seeing color and texture in the wood. I often find a "wood run" to be a creative time. The potential is there for the imagination to come up with some interesting ideas if I take the time to explore.

THE
WORKSHOP WALKAROUND

A collection of wooden bodied hand planes that I've made and use daily in my shop. Clockwise from the left is an 11" long smoothing plane with a 1 3/4" Hock iron. Next is a 9" long smoothing plane with a wooden fence screwed to the bottom. This plane is used for 90 degree edge planing and edge jointing. At the top is a 16" long jointer plane, which is used to level a long surface. The wood is a heavy, dense hardwood from Peru called "quina quina" (pronounced "keyna keyna").

Below, laying on its side, is a round-bottom smoothing plane made of maple with a curved iron, useful for coopering. Beside the round-bottom plane is a 9" long scraper plane, the blade is set at about 95° to the sole and is used to work with very dense or interlocked grained woods.

Below that is a short, 6" long wooden block plane or polishing plane, made of pecan with a 1 1/2" wide cutter. Next is an even shorter polishing plane with a 1 1/4" iron. It measures about 4 1/2" long and is made of tulipwood. At the bottom of the photograph is a small Japanese style trimming plane that measures about 2 1/2" long, it's used for chamfering and getting into tight spaces. The last plane is a 10" long smoothing plane made out of a very beautiful piece of maple.

Starting from the left going clockwise, the first plane is a Stanley #4 smoothing plane. At the top of the photograph, is a #608 Bedrock jointer plane that measures 21" long with a 2 3/8" wide iron. The high level of workmanship makes this pre-1914 plane a treat to use. The next plane is a modern day Record low angle block plane. In the center of the photograph is a brass 4" wide hand router. At the bottom, right hand corner is a Stanley #90 bullnose plane and the final plane in this photograph is a bronze scraper plane made by Lie-Nielsen™. A scraper plane is used for trim work and working with difficult, roed woods that can't be planed with a traditional bench plane.

Traditional Japanese hand tools. Starting with a small hand-broom at the top left corner and working clockwise. At the top of the photograph is a "ryoba" saw. It has cutting teeth on both sides of a very thin flexible blade, one side is for cross cutting while the other side is for rip cuts. Japanese saws cut on the pull stroke and can therefore have very thin blades.

The next tool is a traditional Japanese smoothing plane which measures about 11" long. The plane is made of Japanese red oak with a handmade, laminated steel blade. Beside that is a smaller version of a Japanese smoothing plane which is sometimes called a "polishing plane" with a Japanese white oak body. Like the saws, Japanese planes cut on the pull stoke. Next is a special Japanese plane called a "chamfer" plane, used to put a beveled edge on the corner of a table top or leg.

The next tool is a "boat builders" hammer useful for adjusting plane irons. Next is a Japanese spoke shave, it has a red oak handle and a small laminated cutter capable of doing very fine work. The next five tools in the sequence are Japanese handmade chisels, with laminated steel blades. Next is an awl used for starting drill holes.

In the center of the photograph is a small "dozuki" saw, which means the blade has cutting teeth on only one edge. Beside the small dozuki saw in the middle of the photograph is a flush cutting, wooden nail saw. The last tool is a handmade Japanese dozuki saw. The special teeth make the saw excellent for cutting dovetails.

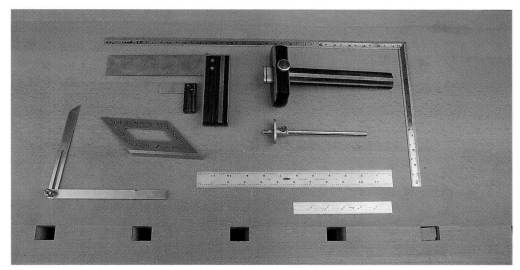

This is a collection of layout tools, both Japanese and Western. Starting left and moving clockwise is a medium sized, Japanese framing square. Next are a pair of marking gauges and 12" and 6" metal rulers. Moving around the circle is an adjustable bevel square, a 45° square, and a pair of 90° squares for laying out joinery.

A 6" long wooden block plane made of pecan along with a Japanese plane adjusting hammer. I've replaced the handle with a hand-shaped piece of osage orange, which fits my hand very comfortably. Tapping on the iron adjusts for a deeper cut, while tapping on the back of the plane body backs out the iron. This block plane can be used with both hands or with one hand.

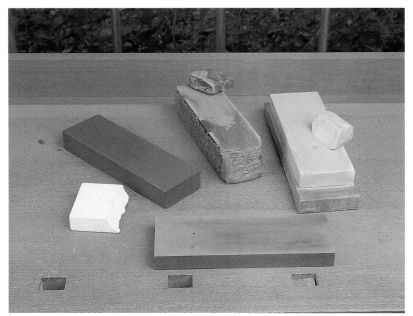

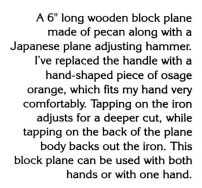

This photograph shows a collection of Japanese water stones. Starting at the top left is a 1200 medium grit, man-made Japanese water stone. To the right is a quarried natural "blue stone" which is approximately 2000 to 2500 grit. Sitting on the blue stone is a "nagura" stone which is rubbed on the blue stone to make a paste or slurry which helps in the cutting process.

The next large bench stone is a man-made, 8000 grit polishing stone. It is used in conjunction with its own nagura, which also serves to create a slurry and aides in the polishing process. At the bottom of this photograph is a fast cutting, 700 grit man-made ceramic water stone, the first I use in the sharpening process. The final stone in the photograph is a broken piece of 6000 grit polishing stone that I use for knives and smaller tools.

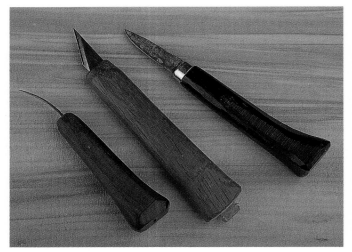

This photograph shows three handmade bench knives. From left to right is a very small knife with a curved blade and cocobolo handle, made for a specific project. The next knife is a 1/2" wide violin maker's blade, made by Ron Hock with a handle made of padauk. The final knife, a gift from my teacher, James Krenov, has a fairly long blade and an ebony handle.

This is a detail photograph of a very special handmade, Japanese dozuki saw. It shows some details of the fine workmanship as well as the signature of the Japanese craftsman that made it.

A shooting board is a jig that is used to hold a workpiece at a right angle, while a 90 degree edge is planed. It's used in conjunction with a hand plane, which is laid on its side and travels along the length of the shooting board. The work piece is held against a stationary cleat at the top of the shooting board, while a finely adjusted plane is used to shave the end of the workpiece at a true 90 degree angle.

The shooting board shown is for a right-handed person. A left-handed person would want to build this jig so that the plane travels along the left-hand side. Note: The side of the hand-plane body needs to be square to the sole of the plane in order to trim the workpiece off squarely.

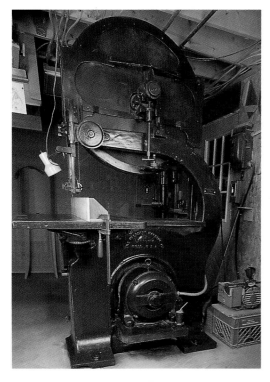

My 1954 36" Crescent bandsaw measures 8' tall and has a three horsepower, three phase motor. Its weight and power allow me to saw very accurate veneers from solid planks up to 16" wide.

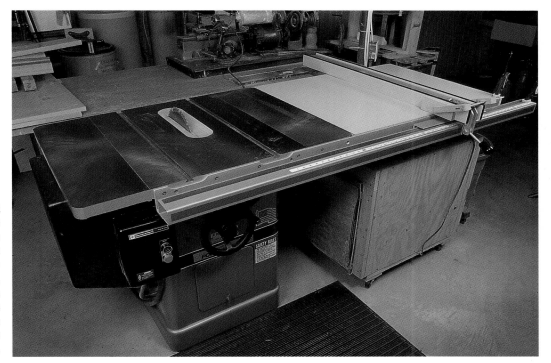

A 10" Powermatic™ cabinet base, table saw with a three horsepower motor and a Biesemeyer™ fence. Also shown in the photograph is a recirculating box below the side table, which is a plywood box with a furnace blower inside that draws air from the shop, through a series of filters, then recirculates clean air back into the shop.

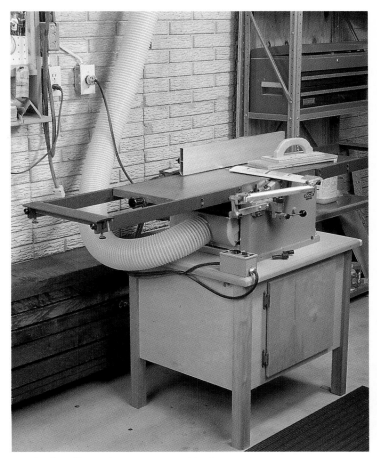

An Inca™ combination jointer/thickness planer made in Switzerland. Shown here in its jointer mode with the outfeed table in place. Combination machines save floor space in a small shop.

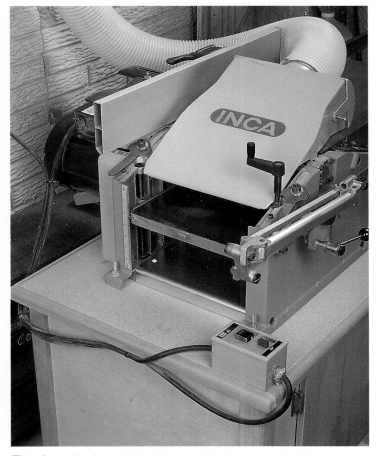

This shows the Inca jointer/planer in the planer mode. The outfeed table is removed and material is sent under the cutter head. I chose the Inca machine for its high level of accuracy and the ease in which I can switch from jointing to planing. The planer can "thickness" veneers to about a 1/16" thick, depending on the wood species.

11

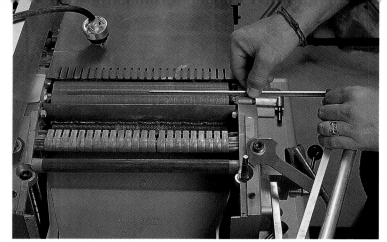

Another feature of the Inca is the ability to quickly change the cutting blades. The doubled-ended, disposable blades are slid out of the cutter head, reversed, and slid back in. Alignment is done by centrifugal force and the entire process of changing to a sharp set of blades takes about 45 to 60 seconds. Notice that the machine is unplugged for blade changes.

A horizontal boring machine. The stand and adjustable mortising table are made by Laguna™ tools. The mortising is done with a three horsepower, variable speed plunge router mounted to the back of the mortising table. The mortising table can be adjusted up and down and travels in and out, left and right while the plunge router remains stationary. I have 1/2", 3/8", and 1/4" collets for the router, which allow me to use a wide range of end mill bits to cut mortises. The end mills are four fluted and center cutting. I use the longer version of these cutters, available from MSC Tools. I've made an auxiliary plywood top that is attached to the mortising table that allows me to do repetitive mortise work. This is important when building something like a coffee table where you have a number of mortises that are exactly the same size and in the same location.

A pair of shop-made saw horses, typical of what I use in my shop. They're light weight and nest together when not in use and can support a surprising amount of weight. I typically use these for organizing project parts, such as in this photograph or for laying out and cleaning up rough lumber as I make lumber selections. I have several pairs of these saw horses, which are all the same height and can be combined when dealing with longer material.

SHARPENING

Sharpening is one of the most important skills required for successful woodworking. Accuracy and enjoyment of the work can often hinge on the craftsman's ability to understand and eventually master this skill. It's not difficult, it just takes practice. It requires that the woodworker pay attention to what is working and what is not with the stone, the steel, and the sharpening process and begins to adjust to that information. I will demonstrate the technique I use. However, I feel there is no one correct way to sharpen. What works for each person is the best method.

I prefer to use Japanese water stones for sharpening plane irons, chisels, and so on. Other choices would be Arkansas or India stones, which use oil as a lubricant. There are also man-made diamond stones and ceramic stones, with which many people have had success. I like Japanese water stones because they cut quickly and use water as the lubricant. A down side is that the stones also wear quickly, often dishing out in the center or along the edges, however they are easily re-flattened. Man-made water stones are widely available and fairly inexpensive, they come in a number of grits or degrees of coarseness. Some common grits useful for a woodworker are an 800 grit coarse stone, a medium 1200 grit stone, and a 6000 grit polishing or finish stone.

Natural stones are mined from various regions of Japan. The intended use and quality of the stone depends on where the stone is acquired. Many experienced craftspeople feel that natural stones perform better. However they can be quite expensive and require some additional care and some getting used to. Especially in the sense that the personality of each individual stone differs a little bit.

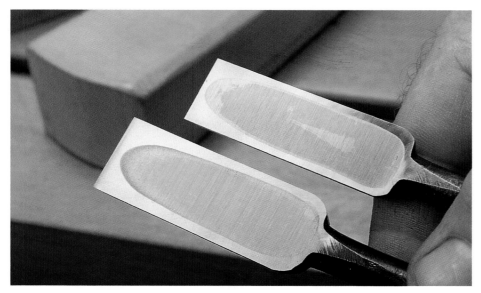

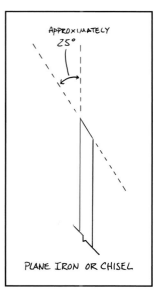

The above photograph shows the bottom, flat side of two Japanese chisels. The Japanese chiselmaker creates a concave area in the bottom, which reduces the area of the hard steel for more efficient flattening. In order for cutting tools to be truly sharp, the flat planes represented by the bevel and the back must intersect. The point in which they intersect is the cutting edge. If the two planes do not intersect as a result of dulling from use or improper sharpening, the cutting edge is not sharp.

The first step in sharpening a new tool is to flatten and polish the back or flat side. The top chisel above has been flattened and polished and has been in use for some time. The bottom chisel is new and needs some attention before it can be used.

Nearly all cutting tools come out of the box in a less than perfect form. Even high quality and expensive planes and chisels are generally not honed and ready for use. I think of these tools as arriving in my hands in a kind of "kit condition." Before I can begin to put them to use, I need to spend some time perfecting and preparing them to create the results I expect.

Before flattening can begin, I need to true up my Japanese water stones. I start with a coarse stone, which in this case is a #700 grit, man-made ceramic stone made by Bester™. I flatten the stone on a piece of plate glass with a sheet of 220 grit wet/dry sandpaper. I spray the sandpaper with water to lubricate it and begin the flattening process. A little water sprayed on the glass helps the sandpaper stay in place.

Move the stone back and forth across the sandpaper, checking its condition once in a while to see that the entire surface is being abraded by the sandpaper. Typically, after a stone has been used for a while it will begin to dish out in the middle. The color of the stone becomes uniform as the high areas are worn down until the stone surface is flat. This can also be confirmed with a straight edge.

Once the coarse 700 grit stone has been flattened, I rinse it off to get rid of any abrasive sandpaper particles. The 700 stone is used to flatten the next stone, in this case, a 1200 grit King brand water stone. The 700 stone levels the high surfaces of the 1200 grit stone, making it perfectly flat. I do this over my stone storage tray or a sink. If the stones begin to stick together, a little water will act as a lubricant

The 1200 grit stone is now used to flatten the next stone, which is the natural blue stone. The blue stone is a nice bridge between medium and polishing stones, reducing the big jump between 1200 grit and 6000 or 8000 grit. The 1200 stone levels any high areas of the blue stone very quickly. Once the blue stone has been flattened, I set it aside and use the same 1200 grit stone to flatten the 8000 polishing stone. The polishing stone's surface is extremely smooth and needs an almost constant trickle of water to keep it from sticking to the 1200 stone. Flattening high quality polishing stones on sandpaper may rough up the surface too much and risk leaving sandpaper particles embedded in the stone's surface.

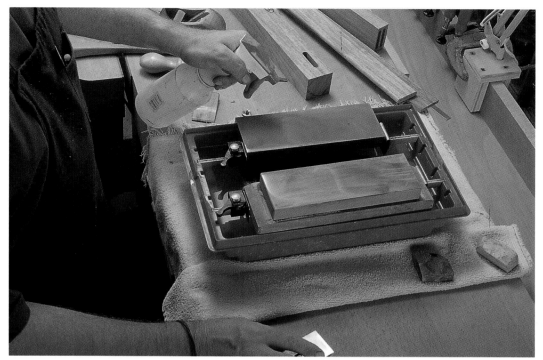

Shown here is my setup for sharpening irons and chisels. The red tray, called a "water pond," stores three or four Japanese water stones which are kept submerged under water when not in use. I use a spray bottle to keep the surface of the 700 stone wet with standing water. I spray the surface of the stones regularly as they absorb water. The water acts as a lubricant and keeps the plane iron or chisel from damaging the stone.

I place the entire flat bottom side of the chisel on the 700 grit stone. I use the fingers from my left hand and the index finger of my right hand to keep the surface of the chisel flush against the top surface of the stone. I move the steel back and forth on the stone for a dozen or so strokes, then check the bottom to see which areas have been affected by the cutting action of the stone. This will quickly tell me how flat the steel is and gives an idea of how much flattening is required before the texture left by the 700 grit stone is apparent on the entire bottom surface. Once the bottom of the chisel has a uniform texture or scratch marks, I rinse it off in the water tray.

I continue using the same technique on the 1200 stone, moving back and forth and in a circular motion. Occasionally checking the progress, I can see that the surface is being refined and polished. The idea is that each finer stone removes the scratches that were left by the previous stone. The texture of the steel becomes different and more polished as you move up through each stone.

I've now replaced the 1200 grit stone with the natural blue stone. Using the same motion and keeping even pressure across the back of the chisel, the back becomes more polished. Once finished, I make sure that I rinse the slurry off the chisel as I switch from stone to stone. This way I don't contaminate a finer stone with the particles from a coarser stone.

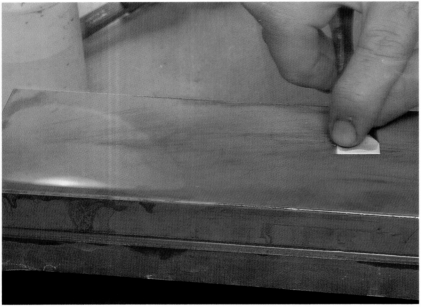

With the scratches from the blue stone consistent and all the way out to the cutting edge, I move to the 8000 grit polishing stone. I use fairly hard pressure to polish out the fine blue stone scratches, using short strokes and moving around the stone for more even wear. The result is a mirror finish. I can see the reflection of my eye when I look at the back. The goal is that the polished back surface is all the way up to the cutting edge. If the surface is less than mirror-like a little distance from the cutting edge, that's all right. The finer the back surface is, the sharper the chisel can become. The nagura stone can be rubbed on the wet surface of the stone, creating a slurry that helps polish and lubricate the stone. The slurry is like a wet paste and can be moved around underneath the blade as required.

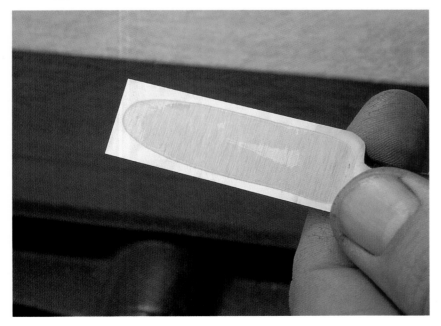

This is the result of time spent flattening the back. The whole process took approximately twenty minutes and is a one time operation. Once the back side has been flattened and polished this way it only needs to be touched up occasionally, never needing to go back to the 700 grit stone and starting over. From now on the bulk of the work happens on the bevel side of the chisel with the polishing stone being the only stone used on the flat back side.

Shows the bevel edge of the same chisel. Notice the shiny cutting edge and the wavy line that separates the harder steel from the softer, dark steel. To prepare the chisel for use, the attention should now be focused on the bevel. This technique is identical to the "Sharpening a Plane Iron" section that follows, with the exception of "hollow grinding the bevel." The bevel is kept flat on a Japanese chisel whereas I prefer to put a hollow grind on plane irons.

The process of sharpening cutting edges, whether they be plane irons or chisels, is basically the same. This section will demonstrate the technique for sharpening a plane iron. Shown is a small wooden plane with an iron that needs to be resharpened. The blade can be backed out of the plane body by tapping on the back of the plane with a small hammer. This loosens the wedge that holds the iron in place.

Remove the breaker from the plane iron.

I use a hand grinder to create a hollow on the bevel side of plane irons. The hollow grind reduces the surface of the bevel itself which allows for very quick sharpening. Here I adjust the wooden jig that the plane iron travels on so that the bevel angle is approximately 25°. A carriage bolt threaded through the base of wooden jig adjusts the angle up and down.

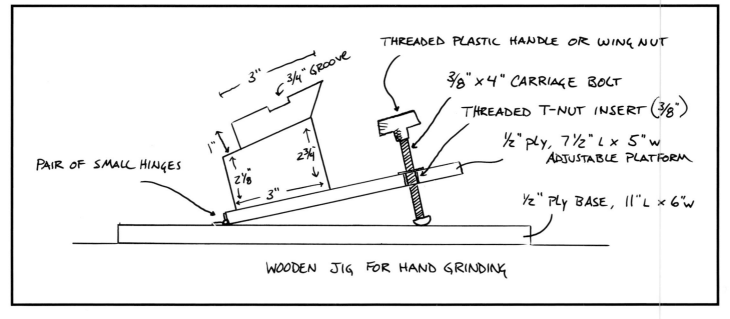

THREADED PLASTIC HANDLE OR WING NUT

3/8" x 4" CARRIAGE BOLT

THREADED T-NUT INSERT (3/8")

1/2" ply, 7 1/2" L x 5" w
ADJUSTABLE PLATFORM

1/2" ply BASE, 11" L x 6" w

3" — 3/4" GROOVE

1"

2 3/4"

2 1/8"

3"

PAIR OF SMALL HINGES

WOODEN JIG FOR HAND GRINDING

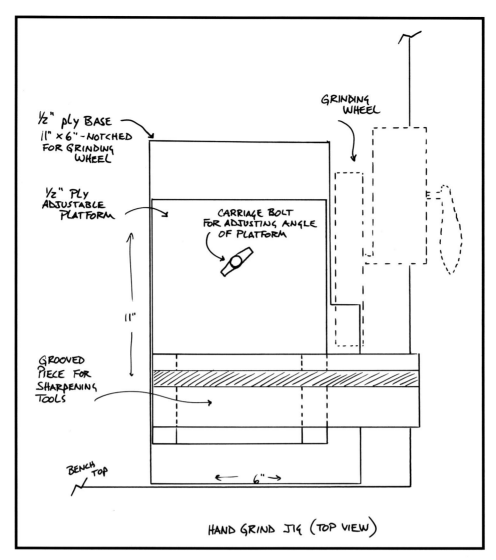

½" ply BASE
11" × 6" – NOTCHED FOR GRINDING WHEEL

½" PLY ADJUSTABLE PLATFORM

CARRIAGE BOLT FOR ADJUSTING ANGLE OF PLATFORM

GRINDING WHEEL

11"

GROOVED PIECE FOR SHARPENING TOOLS

6"

BENCH TOP

HAND GRIND JIG (TOP VIEW)

Once the jig is adjusted to create an approximately 25 degree angle, rotate the grinding wheel a few revolutions to transfer grinding marks to the bevel of the iron. This will give an idea of how much I need to raise or lower the angle of the jig to fine tune the angle.

My right hand rotates the grinding wheel while my left hand holds the iron, moving it back and forth along the spinning wheel. The groove in the wooden jig allows me to positively position my fingertips and move the iron left and right at 90° to the grinding wheel. The black handled bolt shown in front of the wheel is used for raising and lowering the table angle.

Left: A detail shot of the hand position. Fingertips are in the groove of the table controlling the movement of the iron.

Below: With some practice, a very accurate grind can be put on the cutting iron. The cutting edge is very straight and the process took five or six minutes. The beauty of using a hand grinder versus an electric grinder is that the low speed generated by the wheel doesn't allow for heat build-up on the cutting edge. Electric grinders can be used for this but much care must be taken to make sure the steel doesn't get overly hot and turn blue, which means it has lost its temper and will no longer hold a cutting edge. Dipping the steel in water regularly will keep the steel cool.

Place the bevel down on the wet surface of the 700 grit sharpening stone. My right hand supports the bevel, keeping it flat on the stone as shown.

I use the fingertips of my left hand to additionally support the bevel of the iron. The hollow grind makes it easy to know when the bevel is flat on the stone. I move the iron back and forth at a slight angle along the water stone, making sure to make use of the entire surface of the stone rather than concentrating all the wear in one area. Add water to the stone as it dries.

After about a dozen strokes, I check to see the results on the bevel. I can see that the wear is taking place evenly all along the cutting edge. If it weren't, I would go back to the grinder and concentrate on straightening out the grind.

With only a few strokes on the coarse stone, I've created a burr or wire edge on the back of the iron. The burr can easily be felt and seen. Later with the finer stones, it becomes a little more difficult to see and feel. This iron has already been flattened and polished as previously described, so all that's needed now is to remove the burr. This is done on the 8000 grit polishing stone. The nagura stone creates a slurry on the polishing stone surface.

I place approximately 1/2" of the back of the iron on the polishing stone and take 10 or 12 short strokes which will remove the fine burr.

Once the wire is removed, I move on to the 1200 grit medium stone. Spray the surface with water, and using the same finger and hand location as before, keep the bevel of the iron located flat on the surface of the stone.

After 15 or 20 strokes on the 1200 stone, I check the bevel. If I see that the abrasion marks from the coarse 700 stone used previously are gone *and* I've created a new burr on the polished back side, it's time to move back to the polishing stone to get rid of the new burr.

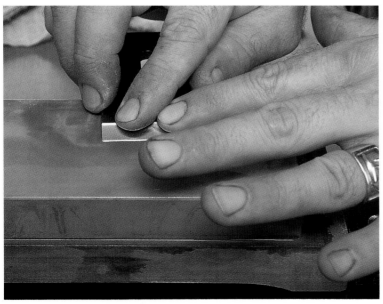

Again, placing approximately 1/2" of the iron onto the polishing stone surface and applying even pressure across the width of the iron, I move the iron back and forth 8 to 10 strokes until I feel that the burr been honed away. I check it with touch and sight to determine if the burr is gone, then move onto the next stone.

The blue nagura stone creates a slurry on the natural blue stone prior to use. It should be mentioned that I store this stone dry. Natural stones are sometimes prone to cracking and I've had good success preserving this one by not keeping it submerged in water. When the stone was new, I wrapped its base in several layers of cheese-cloth, then coated it with a few applications of varnish to aid in holding the stone together.

I generally use the fingertip location shown in this photograph to assure even pressure across the bevel of the iron. This natural stone can wear quickly, so I'm very careful to move it constantly around the surface of the stone, taking fairly short strokes and not concentrating on one area of the stone too much. After a minute or two, I check the bevel to see that the abrasion marks from the previous 1200 grit stone are gone and that I've created a new burr on the flat side.

Again remove the burr on the polishing stone, concentrating on the leading 1/2" of the iron.

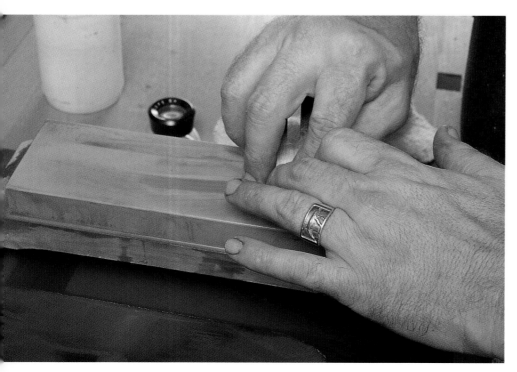

The bevel is now ready to polish to a perfect edge. Using the same finger pressure as before, work around the stone with short strokes. This can take several minutes to remove scratches from the blue stone. The burr created on the back flat side is very fine and difficult to feel. It is sometimes easier to see it in the reflection of a light bulb than it is to feel it with your fingertips. Once I'm beginning to see a polished surface on the bevel, I flip the iron over and work on the flat side. I alternate between bevel and flat side until no indication of a burr is left at the cutting edge. This I usually check by looking for a fine, white line of light reflecting right at the cutting edge under a strong light bulb. The presence of a white line indicates that the bevel and the flat side have not inter-sected at the cutting edge. I continue to work both bevel and flat side on the polishing stone until this fine, white line disappears and reflects no light. You can also check to see if the iron will shave hair off your hand al-though I tend to rely on my eye.

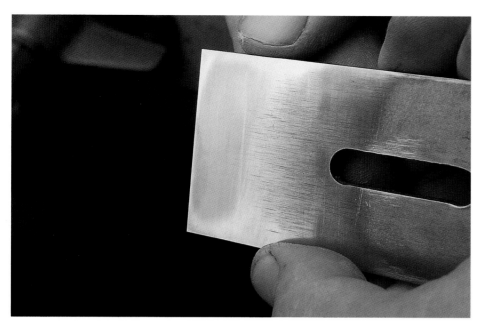

The polished back side of the plane iron.

The bevel side of the iron. The polished cutting edge is easily seen and has no trace of white light reflecting at the edge. Very little steel has been honed away allowing for several sharpenings before the iron needs to be taken back to the hand grinder to re-establish the hollow grind on the bevel.

The breaker is positioned about 1/32 of an inch behind the cutting edge for fine shavings.

The iron and breaker assembly is placed back into the plane.
The plane's wooden wedge is firmly tapped into place against
the iron to hold the assembly in position.

Holding the plane upside down, sight along the plane's sole while
lightly tapping the back of the iron. I tap the blade forward until I can
see a glint of steel barely visible above and parallel with the sole.

SCRAPERS

Many woodworkers think of scrapers as tools for coarse work and removing dried glue. However, a well prepared scraper can take off fine, plane like shavings and produce a surface as smooth as 400 grit sandpaper. Hard, roed woods or those with figure can be discouraging or even impossible to hand plane. Even with a well tuned plane, the results can be frustrating with areas of unavoidable tear out. With these types of woods, leveling and smoothing with a scraper can produce a flawless surface.

I have a number of scrapers of different sizes and thicknesses. The thicker ones are used first for leveling and can remove a lot of material. The thinner, more flexible scrapers can be thought of as finishing scrapers. Use the scrapers at an angle of 45 degrees or higher. If you have to scrape at a lower angle, the burr may be at too steep an angle or you may have used too much pressure with the burnisher. In use, scrapers can be pulled towards or pushed away from you. I find that I get more control and better results when I flex the scraper and push it like a plane.

The first time you use a scraper for several minutes, you'll notice one complaint, your thumbs seem to have caught on fire! Use a refrigerator magnet stuck to the scraper to act as a heat sink. It works surprisingly well. There's also a scraper holder available through woodworking catalogs that helps take the heat and discomfort out of scraping.

The first step in preparing a scraper is to joint the long cutting edge with a 6" mill bastard file. Position the scraper in a vice, sandwiched within a scrap of newspaper to catch the metal fillings. Carefully position the file lengthwise on the edge and at 90° to the scraper's face. Make several passes until the file has removed metal from the entire length of the edge.

"Draw file" the edge by positioning the file at 90 degrees to the scraper and making several full length passes. This refines the edge of the scraper and prepares it for honing on the sharpening stones.

The coarse 700 grit water stone will remove the coarse marks left by the file on the cutting edge. Flex the scraper with your thumb and fingers to help position the scraper at 90 degrees to the surface of the stone. Be careful to move the scraper at an angle across the stone to prevent damaging the stone's surface. The stone can also be turned up on its edge, taking advantage of another surface for sharpening. Scrapers can leave shallow gouges in the stone's surface, so by using stone's edge, the wide surface remains in good condition for plane irons and chisels.

Once the stone has removed the file marks, lay the scraper on its side overlapping the stone by about 1/2". Position your fingertips evenly along the face of the scraper making sure the surface of the stone is wet, move the scraper back and forth and begin honing each face. The idea is to create a 90 degree polished edge on both sides of the scraper. Once the faces and both edges of the scraper have been honed with a coarse stone, repeat the process with the 1200 grit stone. Work the edge of the scraper, flexing the scraper with your hands until the marks left by the coarse stone have been polished away. With the two long edges honed, lay the scraper on its side and work on the faces.

Repeat the steps on a 6000 or 8000 polishing stone, flexing the scraper blade while working on the cutting edge and again evenly spacing your fingertips to apply even pressure when working on the faces. The end result is a polished, 90 degree edge with smooth adjacent faces.

Top: With a scraper held firmly in the vice, a hardened burnisher is used to create a burr or hook on the long edges of the scraper. To create a burr on the left side of the first edge, I begin by moving the burnisher at 90 degrees along the polished edge of the scraper applying medium to hard pressure. After a number of strokes I begin to slowly tilt the burnisher one or two degrees toward the left face while continuing to make passes along its length with the burnisher.

Eventually I arrive at 4 or 5 degrees off of horizontal and have created a burr. This burr, like a plane iron and if sharpened correctly, will create shavings. The burr can now be created on the right side of the cutting edge of the scraper by again starting at horizontal using medium pressure, repeating the process and slowly tilting the burnisher to approximately 4 or 5 degrees to the right of horizontal.

Repeat the process on the other long edge, creating four separate sharpened edges. Experiment with slightly different burnishing angles and pay attention to what works well for you. Once you come up with an angle that works well with the wood species that you are using, make note of your technique and aim for consistency each time you create a burr.

Bottom: Eventually the sharpened burr will begin to break down with use and make dust rather than shavings. Rather than returning to the sharpening stones, a new burr can be created or "laid" with the burnisher. The process takes place on the benchtop with the scraper laying flat. The burnisher is used to lay the previously made burr back out towards the cutting edge. By holding the burnisher at an angle, as shown, and moving along its length with medium pressure, the burr is eliminated so that a new one can be created.

The process of creating the new burr is identical to the way it was created the first time. This process can be repeated four or five times before the cutting edge becomes so serrated that it leaves streaks and an imperfect surface on the wood. At that point it is time to go back to the medium sharpening stone and create a new 90 degree edge, then polish as before. A new burr is then created with the burnisher.

THE
COFFEE TABLE PROJECT

The design I've chosen for the step-by-step portion of this book is the result of working on a number of sketches and ideas. I've long had an interest in the idea of the legs of a piece of furniture extending above the top and many of my sketches included this detail in some fashion. This idea seemed especially promising when considering a low piece like a coffee table which is nearly always viewed from above.

The table I designed is a simple, rectangular piece with some unusual details. I rely on these details to add visual interest. The five-sided legs barely protrude above the veneered top and a small overhang allows the table's base to have a more important role in the overall look of the piece. This design lends itself to exploring different combinations of woods, showcasing beautiful color or grain on the top.

The approach I've taken for this book is to build three different coffee tables; not only for the purpose of making the photography process more efficient, but also to show some options in joinery and different wood color and texture choices. Some of the woods I've cho-sen for the tables need to be worked in very different ways, which has allowed me to show a wider range of techniques and demonstrate the use of some additional tools.

Making the same coffee table out of different combinations of wood colors and textures can give the piece a very different feel. An example of this, which can be seen in the Gallery at the end of the book, is the difference between the walnut and red gum table and the narra and machiche table. The red gum table has a wild, flame pattern in the grain and is oriented with the length of the table top, while the machiche table has a more uniform grain pattern which runs across the width of the table top. To my eye, the grain orientation of the machiche table top creates the illusion of the table being slightly wider and shorter than the lengthwise grain direction of the red gum table, even though the dimensions are the same. These subtle differences are difficult to see in photographs, but they do have an effect on the presence of an object and are worth consideration when making design choices.

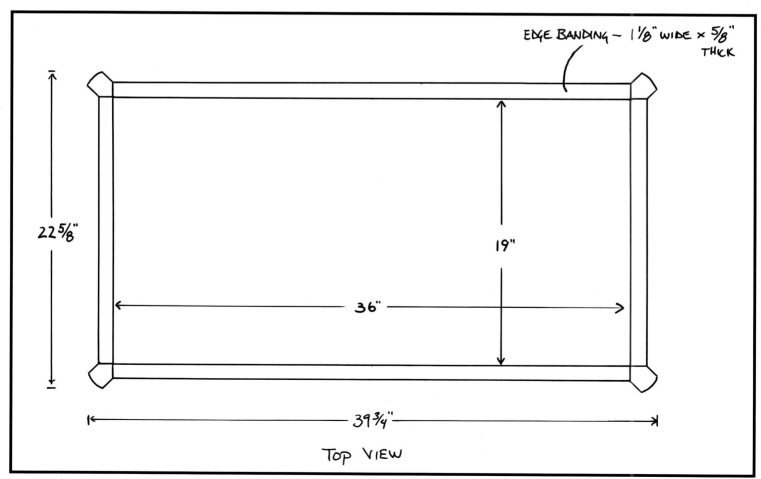

EDGE BANDING — 1 1/8" WIDE × 5/8" THICK

22 5/8"

19"

36"

39 3/4"

TOP VIEW

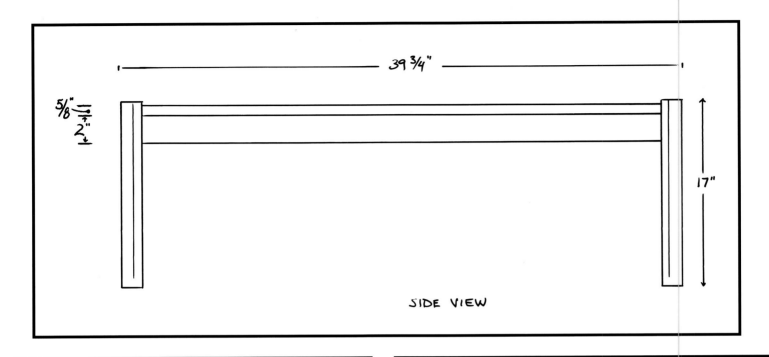

39 3/4"

5/8"

2"

17"

SIDE VIEW

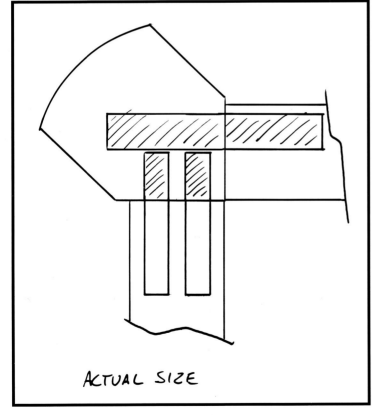

ACTUAL SIZE

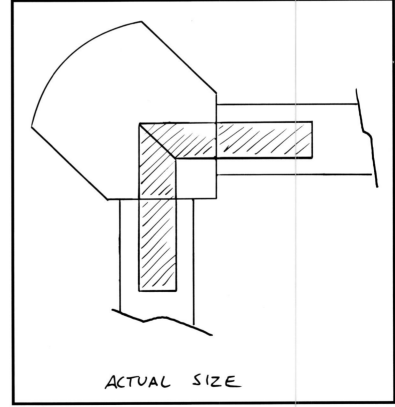

ACTUAL SIZE

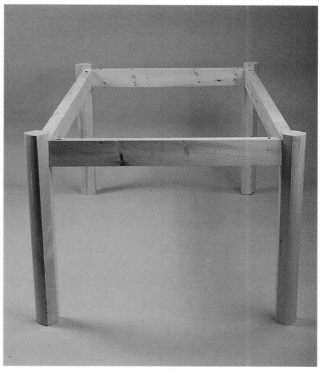

The mockup made of scrap wood with a plywood top notched around the legs and set in place. Held together with screws and hot glue, it can be easily changed to refine the design. The mockup allows me to stand back and view the actual size table from all angles. Each of the four legs differ slightly, which helps to explore possibilities. The mockup helps me to consider many things before committing to the table design, such as dimensions, overall size, relationship of the legs to the frame and top, as well as width and placement of the rails.

One of the most important considerations is the space below the table or the negative space. Another thought is that with only a small overhang of the top, the rail thickness and the top thickness are seen together. This needs to be taken into account when deciding on the width of the rails. I usually live with the mockup for a couple of days, paying attention to first impressions when I walk into the room. Once satisfied with the design, I move onto the real wood.

Using a wooden block plane to clean up the surface of a rough sawn 8/4 plank, I'm able to more clearly see the grain pattern and color of the planks I'm considering. I'm looking for a plank that has fairly straight grain and nice color for the design I've got in mind for this particular coffee table. I've narrowed it down to three or four planks that are likely candidates.

I have selected a pair of planks that measures a full 8/4 (2") and am now beginning to consider the layout by viewing the end grain. The orientation of the growth rings in these planks lend themselves to the five-sided leg detail in the table design.

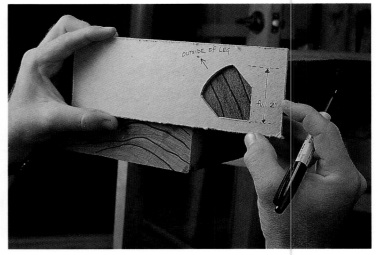

The profile of the leg design shown here in a cardboard template, shows the orientation of the grain which will most likely produce the desired effect that I'm looking for. The idea is to eliminate flat sawn areas on the leg surfaces. This is very manageable on four-sided legs, but a little challenging with a five-sided leg design. Sometimes it is unavoidable to have one of the five sides show flat sawn grain. A flat sawn pattern will often have grain lines and graphics that can sometimes be distracting in the overall leg design.

This 8/4 plank of kwila, an ecologically harvested wood from Papua, New Guinea, illustrates typical growth rings likely to be encountered when selecting wood for a project. The log that this plank came from was large enough to produce rift sawn growth rings across most of its width. The cardboard template greatly aides the ability to see how these growth rings will affect the outcome of the leg. The leg profile template helps to confirm that all five sides will have straight grain rather than flat grain. This adds greatly to the illusion that I'm trying to create of nice straight even legs. With a five-sided leg, the section of the plank that is approaching flat sawn also exhibits grain that is not parallel to any of the five sides.

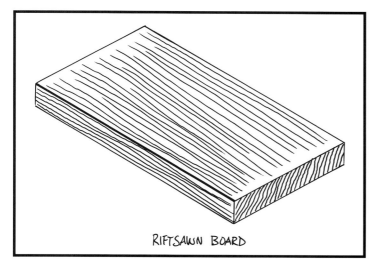

RIFTSAWN BOARD

QUARTER SAWN BOARD

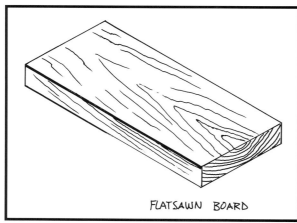

FLATSAWN BOARD

Also of importance is choosing a plank that has fairly straight grain on the face and the 8/4 edge. All of these factors—end grain, the edge grain, and the face grain are considered equally in choosing what section of a particular plank is going to be used for the legs.

As mentioned in the introduction, I'm making more than one table at a time in order to demonstrate a wider variety of techniques. Early on in the book I'll be working on table frames made out of kwila and narra, woods from Papua, New Guinea.

This slide shows laying out the narra plank to get the parts that I need for the project. I've laid out a pair of legs end to end and side by side with chalk, this gives me four legs out of a very similar section of the plank so they will be fairly close in their grain pattern. This plank is approximately 7" wide and allows for the long rails to be placed beside the four legs. The rough length of each leg will be 18" long which allows for room to trim to final length. In addition to the combined length of the pair of legs, I like to add 4" to account for planer snipe.

Planer snipe occurs as the stock enters and exits a thickness planer and results in a short area that is thinner than the rest of the board. This additional 4" brings our length up to 140". The extra length also gives me the luxury of having each leg a couple of inches longer than necessary in case I encounter something unusual, like a knot in the grain pattern. The long rails are also cut an additional 4" to allow for planer snipe, which also brings the rough rail length to 40".

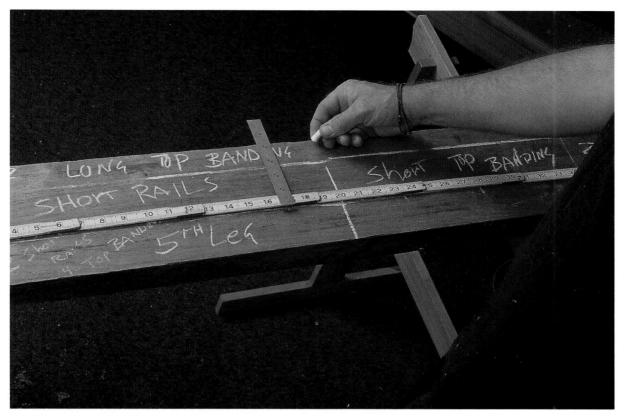

Next, I have laid out a fifth leg at the end of the original four legs. If there is enough material, I always lay out a fifth leg which becomes an extra in case the grain pattern in one of the other four legs is less appealing or a mistake is made during future stages of the project. I lay out the short rails, which have a rough length of 20", as well as material for the edge banding of the top. These edge banding pieces are cut oversized for now and will be milled closer to their final dimensions later in the project. As with the previous laid out section of the board, I've allowed for planer snipe.

Using a double-sided ryoba saw, I cross cut the plank on the layout line to make the mill work more manageable.

Before running planks over the jointer, I determine the grain direction of each section. A pencil mark exaggerates the angle of the grain and tells me at a glance which direction to move the board over the jointers knives in order to cut with the grain.

Initial planing to flatten one face and one edge of the board sections. The planer's cutter guard helps prevent any accidents.

Joint one edge of each plank at 90 degrees to the jointed face.

Tools needed to set up the drift of the bandsaw blade and prepare the saw for resawing. The first step to accurate resawing on the bandsaw is setting up and adjusting the saw. The proper blade is important and I use a sharp 1/2" blade, with 4 hook teeth per inch. The benefit of using a blade with 3 or 4 teeth per inch is that it efficiently removes a lot of material quickly, yet the teeth don't have an overly aggressive set.

Remove the blade currently on the saw. Dust any sawdust off the bandsaw tires and back the guide blocks and thrust bearings away from the blade. Install the 1/2" blade approximately in the center of the tires. The teeth will be pointed down towards the saw table and facing you as you stand in front of the saw. Tension the upper wheel until the blade becomes slightly taut, then rotate the upper wheel by hand for several revolutions. This allows the blade to properly track or find its proper location on the saw's wheels. Adjust the tension

of the blade according to the scale on your particular bandsaw. The blade should be very tight; not so much that you risk damaging the saw, but tight enough to prevent the blade from wandering while in the middle of a cut.

Adjust the upper guide blocks so that they come forward to the back of the blade's gullet and in until they lightly touch the sides of the blade. Tighten the guide blocks in place.

Adjust the upper thrust bearing forward until it lightly touches the back of the blade. Tighten the thrust bearing in place. The bearing should move slightly from light contact with the blade as the blade rotates. The bearing should not be in such tight contact with the blade that it can not be stopped with finger pressure while the blade is being rotated by hand.

Repeat the above two steps to adjust the lower guide blocks and thrust bearing below the saw table. Rotate the blade by hand to double check that both the upper and lower guide blocks and thrust bearing are properly positioned.

The next important step is the find the "drift" of the blade. Band saw blades rarely cut perpendicular to the front of the saw table, so it's important to find each blade's angle at which it naturally wants to cut. Draw a line along the length of a piece of thin scrap wood, parallel to one side.

Turn the saw on and pushing from the end of the scrap, cut part way along the pencil line manipulating the scrap to allow the blade to follow the line. Hold the scrap piece still and turn off the saw.

While still holding the scrap piece in place, place an adjustable bevel square along the front edge of the bandsaw table. Adjust the square's arm against the edge of the scrap piece parallel to the pencil line. Tighten the bevel square. The bevel square's angle now represents the drift of the saw blade.

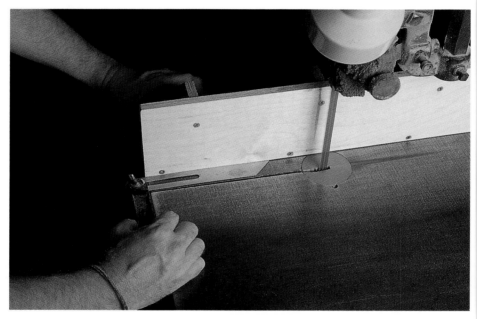

Any time the bandsaw fence is required, the preset bevel square allows the fence to be positioned according to the blade's drift.

With the fence set according to the drift, clamp the fence to the bandsaw table, front and back, at 2 1/16" from the blade.

Turn the saw on and with the jointed face down and the jointed edge against the fence, lightly touch the workpiece to the moving blade.

This will leave a shallow cut that can be measured to double-check the position of the fence.

With a steady feed rate, move the workpiece through the blade. Position your hands so that you don't pause to reposition your grip.

41

Left: BEWARE at the end of the cut that your fingers are not in the path of the blade!

Below left: Back to the jointer to lightly joint the freshly sawn edge of the plank.

Below right: Cut the next pair of legs. With the same bandsaw fence set up, I cut the fifth leg out of the other portion of the plank.

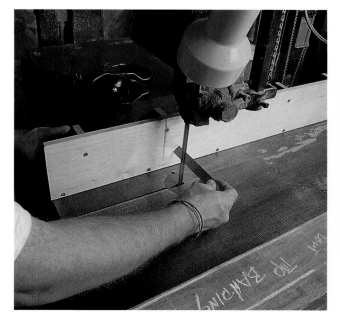

Reset the fence to cut both long and short rails at approximately 2 3/8". Again, use the bevel square to set the bandsaw fence at the correct drift angle.

Rip the long and the short rails using a steady feed rate and being aware of the position of your hands. The remaining materials from these planks will be used for the edge bandings of the table top and can be set aside for now.

Before running each of the table parts over the jointer again, this is a good time to double check the grain direction by looking at both edges of each part. The reason for needing to rejoint after the sawing of the parts has been completed is that often times the built in tension in a plank will release itself when the bandsaw makes its cut. What was a previously flat surface that had been run over the jointer, has sprung slightly. The best thing to do is to let the table parts set overnight. This allows the freshly exposed wood surfaces to acclimate to the shop and can be safely rejointed the following day. If the plank seems to have a lot of tension in it and it springs as it leaves the bandsaw blade, it maybe best to allow the material to set for a week to settle down. Here I draw a series of reference lines on the surface to confirm the entire face has been contacted by the jointers cutters.

Rejoint one edge and one face of each of the table parts. That is legs, rails, and edge bandings.

Next I reset the bandsaw fence to resaw the long and short rails roughly in half. The 8/4 stock measures roughly 2 1/4" thick, so I set the fence at a shy 1 1/8", with the jointed face against the fence and the jointed edge against the bandsaw table.

Using a steady feed rate, I rip the long and short rails. Always be aware of hand positions!

The freshly resawn short rails exposing the new grain pattern.

As the work pieces get smaller in dimension, I use a push block to keep my hands away from the jointer's dangerous cutting head.

With the new face jointed, I rotate the work piece up on its edge and re-establish a new jointed edge. Notice the position of my hands which are well away from the cutter head, as well as the presence of a safety guard that prevents contact with the spinning cutter head.

Above: A long rail with a rejointed face and edge, the grain direction has been redrawn on the freshly jointed edge as well as a little symbol that tells me that this edge has been jointed. The symbol is the letter "J" with a circle around it.

Right: Up until now the mill work has been performed on the narra plank, here I rip long and short rails for the kwila table. The band saw fence is again set at 2 3/8" from the blade.

The freshly sawn
kwila rail is rejointed
along its face.

Above: The freshly
jointed face of one of the
kwila rails showing very
straight grain. With a
smooth surface left by
the jointer, it's easy to tell
the grain direction for
jointing the edge.

Right: Jointing the edge.
Notice the position of
both hands safely away
from the cutter head
with the cutter safety
guard in place.

With the jointing work completed on the kwila parts,
I draw the jointed symbol on the surface. I also draw
a grain direction slash line for future work.

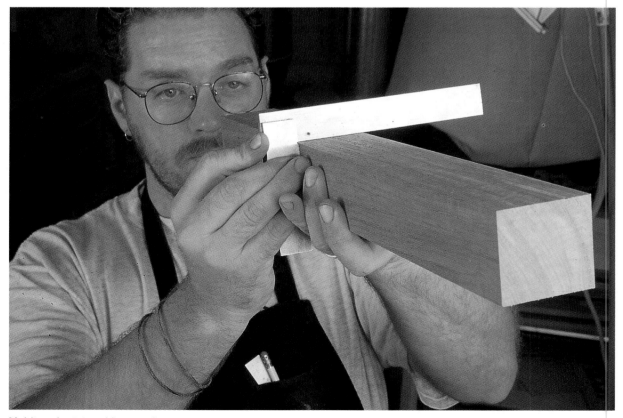

Holding the jointed leg stock up to my eye and aiming it at a light source, I
check the two jointed surfaces for squareness. If light is visible beneath the
blade of the square, the leg stock will need another light pass over the jointer
to correct it. Check the jointer's fence for squareness to the table and adjust if
necessary. Lightly rejoint one of the edges and check again with the square.

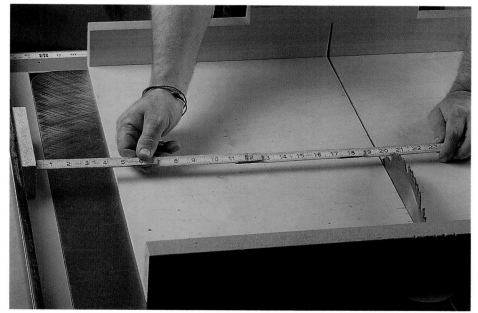

Once all the table base stock has been jointed on two adjacent surfaces, the leg stock and the rail stock can be cut closer to the final length. The leg stock is around 40" long at this stage, so I'll cut each piece in half or 20" long. I use a cut-off box for all cross-cuts on my table saw. Here I hold the ruler up against a plywood scrap which will be clamped to the saw's fence and used as a stop block.

With the fence positioned and locked down, I clamp the stop block to the fence so that it can be used to accurately position each of the pieces to be cut.

With the leg stock in place on the cut-off box, I slide the leg over to the stop block.

Place hands far from the path of the blade, turn on the saw, and while holding the work piece tight against the cut off box fence carefully move the work piece through the blade. The free space between the leg and the table saw fence that is created by the thickness of the stop block prevents the work piece from binding in the blade.

With all the legs and rails cut to within a few inches of their final length, I'm ready to convert my Inca machine to its thickness planer mode. This takes less than 60 seconds and I'm quickly ready to thickness plane the table parts. I check each piece for its grain direction and if I have not already marked a grain direction line as a reference, I do so now. I turn on the planer and the dust collector it's hooked up to and adjust the planer's bed to approximately the thickness of the thickest rough-sawn leg.

I feed the first leg into the machine and raise the bed height until I hear the wood being planed. It takes a few passes before the cutters are removing material from each of the legs. After making a pass with the first jointed side down on the jointer bed, I rotate the leg and make the second pass with the other jointed side down. While keeping an eye on each leg's thickness, I continue planing the legs, raising the bed after each round until they are identical.

If you have the luxury of starting with stock that is a little more than two inches thick, you can stop the legs at a thickness of two inches. It's more common to find lumber that has been milled two inches to begin with, in this case stop planing the planks once all the legs are consistent. You should aim at around 1 7/8", although it may be a little bit less. The only danger in going thinner than that is the legs begin to look a bit thin in relation to the table design after you've cut them to their five-sided profile. In other words, I'm starting thick because the legs are five-sided, not because all coffee table legs need to begin with extra thick stock.

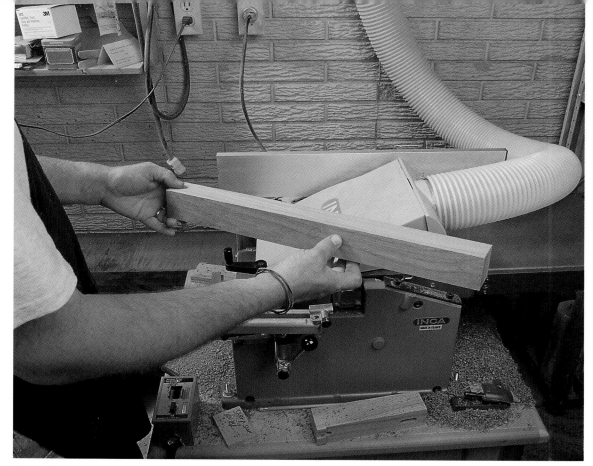

Earlier I brought up the topic of planer snipe and should address it again here. Snipe is an unavoidable occurrence when using a conventional thickness planer. However, with some machines, it's less of an issue than with others. One of the benefits that I enjoy with my Inca jointer-planer is minimal snipe both in depth as well as in length. The snipe occurs as a work piece is being fed into and then exits the cutter head. There is a distance of about 2" where the work piece only has downward pressure from one of the two feed rollers, both entering and exiting. Until both feed rollers are engaged, the work piece can vibrate, which produces a slightly dipped cut that is called "Snipe."

The Inca's feed rollers are placed close together and are made of metal so there's no give or cushioning between the rollers and the wood, which could lead to a more pronounced snipe. Considering the legs of this table, having snipe at the ends of each won't affect any future work or the quality of the craftsmanship. All mortise and tenon joinery will take place on the two jointed surfaces while the two planed surfaces will be sawn off when the legs are cut to their five-sided shape.

Once the legs have been planed to their final thickness, I move on to the four rails. I check each piece for its grain direction and adjust the planer bed to the approximate thickness of the rails. I send the pieces through the machine until they've all been milled to approximately 1" thick and 2 1/4" wide. This allows for strong joinery at the legs while the 2 1/4" width has a pleasing proportion when the table is viewed as a whole.

The completed legs and rails all planed to their final thickness, all surfaces are squared to each other. Notice there are five legs.

I'm now ready to move on to the table saw where I'll cross cut all of the pieces that make up the table's frame to final length. The wooden cut-off box is a fixture that again is used for all straight table saw cuts. It's highly accurate and very safe, allowing me to keep my hands a good distance from the blade. To begin cross cutting I place a stop block against the table saw's fence adjusting the fence until the distance from the stop block to the blade is exactly 17 1/2", the final length of the legs.

After locking the fence in place, I slide the stop block towards my end of the fence. I clamp the block in place using a wooden cam clamp. The stop block is only used to position the work piece.

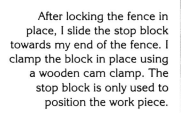

Above: Next, I adjust the height of the blade until it protrudes above the work piece by about 1/8" of an inch.

Right: With the jointed edges down on the cut off box and against the cut off box fence and using a wooden cam clamp to securely position the leg in place, I trim approximately 1/4" off of the 20" long leg.

53

Above: Holding the leg up to a light source and using a cabinet maker's square, I check to see the accuracy of the table saw cut. I check from both jointed surfaces. This will tell me if the table saw blade is 90° to the table as well as the relationship of the cut off box fence being 90° to the face of the table saw blade.

Right: With the results being accurate in both directions, I replace the leg on the cut off box, jointed sides again down on the surface and against the cut off box fence and slide the leg up against the stop block. A cam clamp holds the leg securely against the fence.

With my hands safely out of the way, I move the leg across the moving blade, cutting the leg off squarely to its final length. Notice the space between the leg and the fence, which represents the thickness of the stop block. This space prevents any binding of the workpiece between the blade and fence.

In preparation for cutting the rails to final length, apply tape to the bottom side of the area that will pass over the table saw blade to prevent splintering. The tape that I am using is called "long mask painters tape," this roll happens to be made by 3M™. It comes off easily, and leaves no residue on the wood surface, even under the pressure of clamps.

The first end of the rail is cut off square. A cam clamp keeps the workpiece in place.

The rail is slid against the repositioned stop block, which is clamped in place 19" from the table saw blade. The work piece is cut to final length. Hands are well away from the blade.

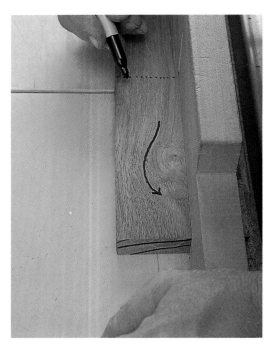

Left: This swirled grain shown here is a pattern that I feel would take away from the finished table design. Because the stock was cut long to start with, I have the luxury of cutting it off. With all the rails cut to final length, the masking tape can be carefully removed.

Below: I like to shoot the ends of each rail on the shooting board, as described earlier, to make them precisely square. Here I'm using a metal jointer plane to do the shooting. One end of the rail is held tightly against the fence and the plane. The plane is moved along the shooting board trimming the rail perfectly square.

Check the end for squareness, both along its width and its thickness. Once satisfied, flip the rail over and shoot the opposite end.

Repeat the process for the second short rail. After both ends are trimmed, check to make sure that both rails are of identical length. Shoot the longer one if necessary.

Now it's time to decide which side of each rail will face out. By looking at each rail's grain pattern, an aesthetic decision can be made. For instance, if I've planned all along to have an upward arc in each rail, I can compare the faces and choose those that create the sense of movement I want. These decisions don't usually happen accidentally, they're the result of careful planning when choosing, laying out, and milling the planks. Blue tape marked with the top of a cabinetmakers triangle tells me at a glance where each rail belongs

MORTISE AND TENON JOINERY

With a rail clamped vertically in a bench vise, the joinery can be laid out. In order to gain slightly longer tenons, the mortises are not centered in the thickness of the rail. The mortise sets in 3/16" from the outer face of each rail. Use a marking knife to transfer the location, then over 3/8" to mark the other side of the mortise.

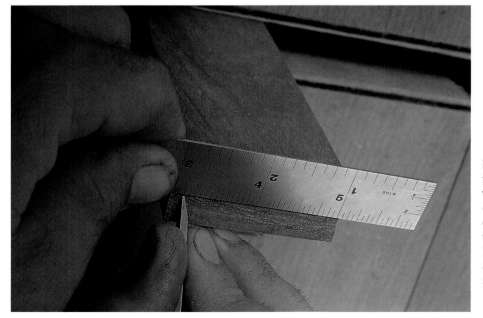

Repeat the layout process, finding the center of the width of the rail. From center, measure out 1 7/8" each way and mark with the knife. The marking knife leaves a fine cut allowing for more accurate set up of the router.

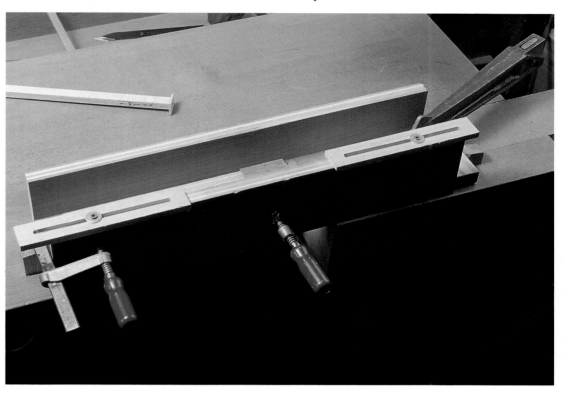

Right: This simple router jig allows for accurate mortising on both rails and legs with a minimum of set up. It's a U-shaped plywood box that uses various stops to position the work piece and the router. The jig is shown with a rail already clamped in place vertically.

Below left: The rail is held square to the box by the square ended plywood stop block shown in the foreground. The work piece sticks up through the bottom of the jig and is raised until flush with the top of the box, then clamped in place.

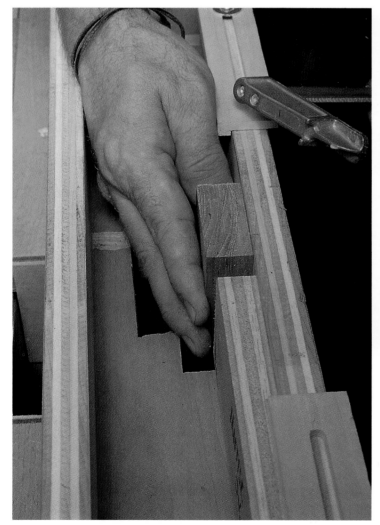

I use an Elu 3 horse power variable speed plunge router for mortising. The router has a fine tuning knob on the fence which allows for accurate adjusting. The cutter is a 3/8" center cutting end mill bit which produces very clean mortises. I've come to prefer them over spiral router bits.

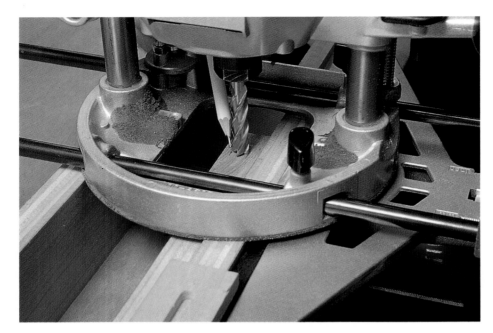

With the router unplugged and the rail clamped in position flush with the top of the box, adjust the router fence until the end mill lines up precisely with the knife layout marks.

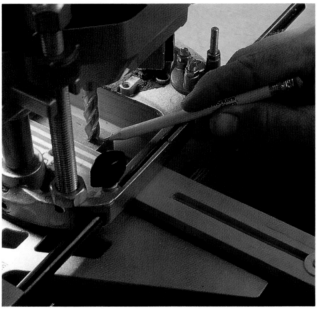

To adjust for the length of the mortise, slide the router to the right lining up the end mill with the layout mark.

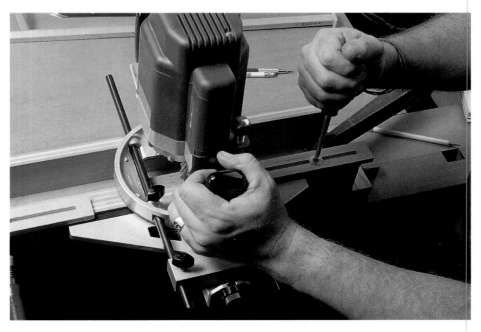

Once in position, tighten the adjustable stop against the router base.

Repeat the steps for the opposite side.

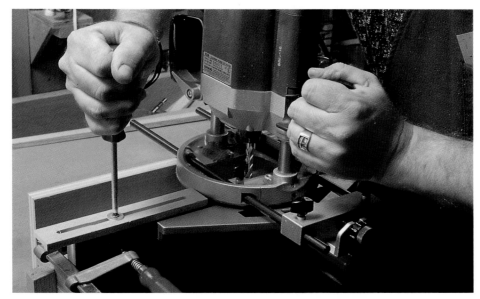

Tighten the second adjustable travel stop against the router base.

All that remains is to adjust the depth of cut. The method of adjustment, of course, varies with each brand of router. First, with the router still unplugged, bottom out the end mill against the end of the rail. Then adjust the plunge stop to the desired depth. These mortises will be 1 3/16" deep.

Here's what the set up looks like ready to go.

With the fence positioned against the mortise box, make a shallow pass from left to right. Traveling in this direction allows the rotation of the end mill bit to aid in keeping the fence riding against the box. Traveling in the opposite direction risks the cutter forcing the fence away from the box spoiling the mortise. The shallow pass allows for making any adjustments in the stops or the fence if the mortise is not exactly where you intended.

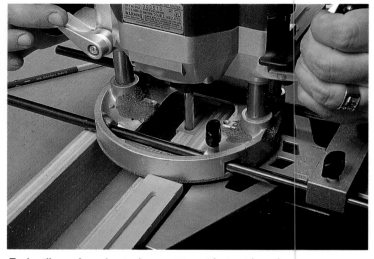

End mills perform best when cutting side to side rather than plunging a series of deep holes. I usually plunge the cutter about 1/8" then move the router left to right. Slide the router back to the left side, plunge another 1/8" and repeat the process until the cutter is at full depth.

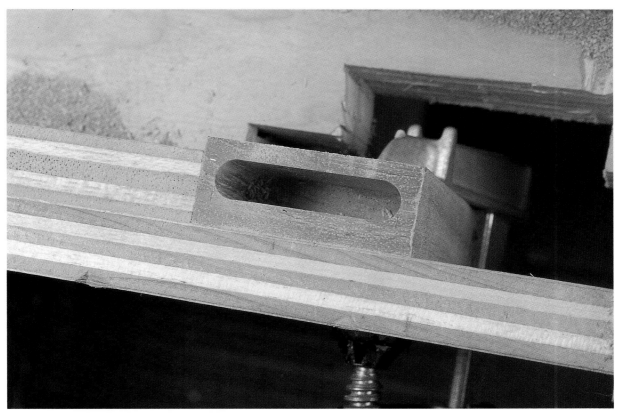

The completed mortise. The end mills I use
are 4-fluted, and leave a very clean cut.

Rotate the rail end for end being sure to keep
the same face against the mortising box so the
mortises are located the same at each end.
Place the rail flush with the top of the box.

Mortise the remaining long and short rail ends.

The drawing of the leg profile helps to envision the future look of the leg. The joinery surface will measure 1 3/16" across after the leg is cut. Transfer this dimension to the leg at the approximate area where the joinery will be. The second mark represents the step in from the edge of the leg to the outside of the rail. This offset is 1/8".

The rail temporarily in position on the leg helps visualize where the mortise will go.

Carrying the edge of the mortise down to the surface of the leg provides a layout mark for setting up the router.

A story stick is created to consistently and accurately transfer the mortise location to the legs. The stick is a straight piece of wood, cut off square at one end. A small scrape is glued and tacked at one end to serve as a cleat. The length of the mortise is laid out at the proper location. The location takes into account the distance from the edge of the mortise to the edge of the rail, the thickness of the finished top and the distance the top of the leg protrudes over the surface of the table top.

Hook the story stick cleat over the top of the leg and knife mark the top and the bottom of the mortise. The width of the rail is represented on the story stick by the dotted lines. With a small square, knife a more visible line the approximate width of the mortise. The mortise location is shown with the X. The pencil lines to the right near the top of the leg represent the thickness of the top.

Slide plywood shims into the mortise box to elevate the leg near the top of the box. The mortise will be more accurate if the router stops are left in position and the leg is moved left and right until the leg marks line up with the end mill cutter. The router fence can be adjusted to locate the end mill to the other knife marks. Once in place, clamp the leg to the box and position and clamp a plywood stop against the top of the leg for easy placement of the next leg.

Because this mortise ties into another mortise coming in from the adjacent side, the depth of each mortise is the same. Take a shallow pass from left to right.

Seen from the other side the test mortise looks good. The clamped plywood stop is visible against the top of the leg.

Rout the mortise taking shallow passes.

Completed mortise. Rout this mortises on each leg, including the extra leg, before moving onto the adjacent mortises. This step will require relocating the plywood stop block.

Using the story stick, transfer the mortise location to the adjacent jointed side.

Left: Position the leg in the mortise box and clamp in place.

Below left: Clamp plywood stop against the top of the leg.

Below: Rout the mortise. When you get 3/8" from the bottom of the cut, the end mill will enter the previously routed mortise.

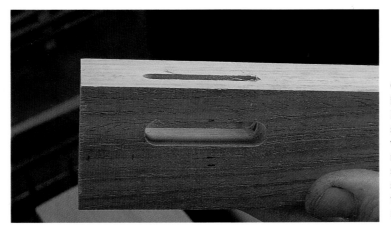

Careful set up has resulted in crisp accurate mortises. Had the depth of cut been set to deep, the end mill would have over cut and removed material that should serve as a glue surface for the adjoining tenon. Cut the remaining mortises.

As an alternative to routing mortises with a hand held router, I also use a horizontal boring machine. The boring machine consist of a heavy metal stand with the mortising table attached to it. The mortising table travels in and out, and left and right on steel rods. The movement is controlled with a pair of joysticks. The height of the table is adjusted with a hand crank and locked in position.

The table has built in stops to limit the travel in all directions and the workpiece is secured to the table with a heavy cam clamp. Attached to the back side of the stand is a plunge router mounted horizontally. As with the hand held router technique, the mortising is done with end mill bits. I use long and extra long end mills for most mortising.

I've modified the table by fitting it with a plywood top. The top has a pair of grooves running across its width and length on which travels a wooden sled with an attached fence. The auxiliary top improves the versatility of the machine, allowing me to do accurate, repetitive mortises. The benefit of this setup is especially noticed when working on something like a set of chairs where several dozen mortises are needed, but it also proves helpful when working on a project like a coffee table.

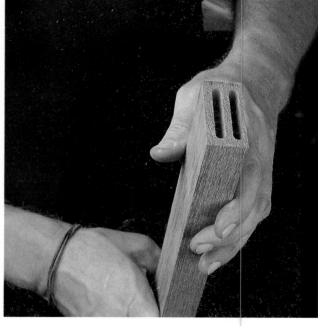

When routing double mortises, a helpful hint is to adjust the height of the mortising table to the top or upper mortise. Once the mortise is routed, slide a wood shim of appropriate thickness underneath the workpiece, elevating it for the second mortise. This technique allows you to move back and forth between the upper and lower mortises without having to change the mortise table height. I've found that once the table height has been changed, it's difficult to reposition precisely.

Likewise, if the rail is stepped in from the inside corner of the leg, the rail can be shimmed 1/8" or whatever is appropriate, eliminating the need to reposition the table height.

Left: With the mortises complete the spline tenons can be made. The mortises will serve as a gauge for getting a good tenon fit. Set up the bandsaw fence to resaw approximately 7/16" from the blade and according to the predetermined blade drift. Extra narra and kwila were set aside earlier for spline tenon stock.. This table only requires eight tenons, however, it's a good idea to make extra stock. Resaw with a steady feed rate and use a push stick if necessary.

Below left: Send the tenon stock through the thickness planer paying attention to grain direction. The extra tenon stock is sent through first to make fine tuning adjustments. As I sneak up on the fit, I test the extra piece into the mortise until it fits snuggly. Finally send the real tenon stock through the planer for its final pass. Thicknessing tenon stock can also be accomplished with a drum sander.

Below right: Test fitting tenon stock. If the planer creates much snipe, the fit can be thrown off. It maybe helpful to trim off any snipe before final fitting.

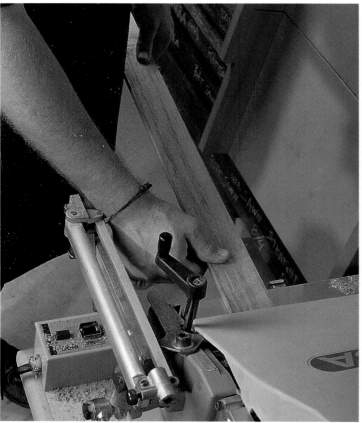

Left: Up until this point the tenon stock has been wider than necessary. Adjust the table saw fence to cut slightly wider than the mortise. Adjust the blade height to just above the thickness of the stock and using a push stick, rip to final width.

Below left: Check the width of stock. It should just start to enter the mortise.

Below right: Tilt the table saw fence to 45 degrees and lower the blade until it protrudes only 1/16" or so above the table top. Position the fence so that the blade is located at about 3/4 of the tenon stock width. Make a test pass on the extra stock. The blade should cut a 1/16" deep groove down the length of the stock. This is to provide an exit for escaping air that might otherwise be trapped at the bottom of the mortise when the tenon is being glued into place. Rotate the tenon stock and cut two grooves on each side.

Here the V grooves can be seen. A medium sized variable speed plunge router clamped upside down in a bench vise serves as a small router table. A 3/16" round over bit is used to rout a radius along all four edges of the 3/8" tenon stock. A hardwood fence clamped to the router base is positioned flush with the router bit guide bearing.

Working from right to left the stock is kept against the fence as the work piece is passed against the cutter. Repeat on all four sides.

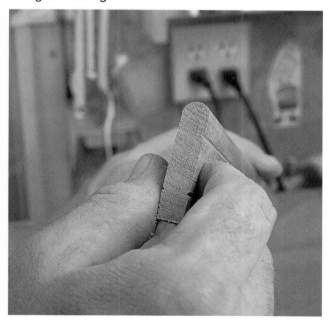

One radiused edge.

If the tenon fits a little too snuggly in the mortise, a couple of light plane strokes along one edge will reduce its width. This edge is then taken back to the router table to round over again.

Test for snug fit. I aim for a fit that can be pushed in by hand with no play. If the tenon requires a mallet, it's too tight.

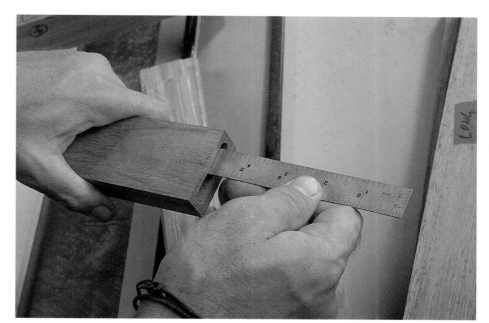

After combining the depth of the rail and leg mortises, I subtract approximately 1/16". This allows for a collection of glue in the bottom of the mortise after the joint has been clamped together.

The length of the tenon after subtracting 1/16" is 1 15/16". Position the stop block on the table saw cut off box and clamp into place.

I use a pencil eraser to keep pressure on the tenon piece while cutting. This prevents the tenon from being trapped and wedged between the blade and the stop block. Once the cut-off box is retracted from the blade, I use the pencil to slide the tenon out of the way.

Left: Finished tenons, with a couple to spare.

Below: Ease the edges of the tenons with a woodworking file. This also provides a space for glue build up in the bottom of the mortise.

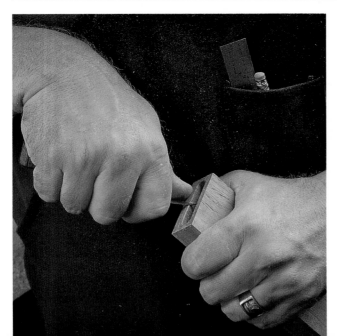

A knife is an efficient tool for easing the edges of the mortise. This eased edge provides space for the glue to squeeze out of the tenon and build up around the base of the tenon where it joins the shoulder of the rail.

While cutting tenons, I cut the extra tenon stock piece into short test fit tenons. They measure 1 1/2" long and will be used while dry fitting the table. They are long enough to hold the table together without getting in the way of the section of the mortise where the tenons will eventually be mitered to a final fit.

With the joinery complete, the legs can be cut to a final shape.
The sketches help determine some joinery possibilities.

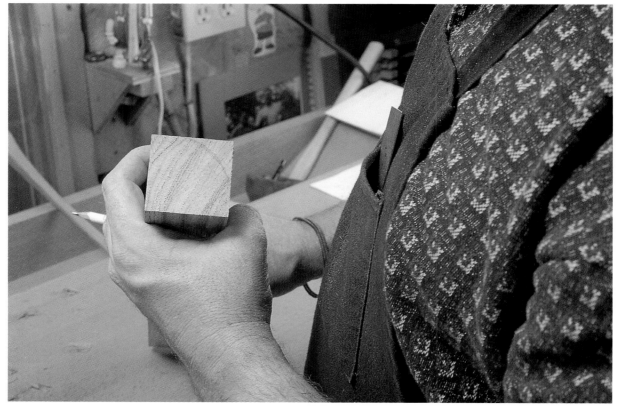

Here's the five sided profile sketched on the end of a
leg to help visualize the areas that need to come off.

Working from the inside corner of the leg, measure over 1 3/16" each way. The line represents the first 45 degree face or side of the leg.

A 45 degree square accurately locates the marks.

The layout complete, with the mortise location penciled in place. The distance from the inside corner diagonally to the outside face of the leg is approximately 2 1/16".

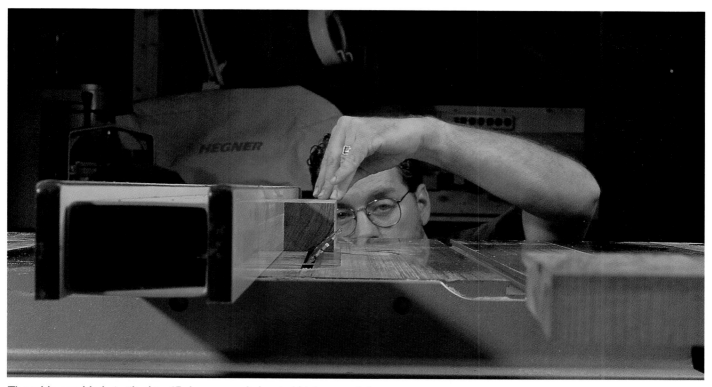

The table saw blade is tilted to 45 degrees and elevated high enough to remove the outside corner of the leg. The fence is adjusted so the pencil mark lines up with the blade. The blade I'm using for this cut is a 24 tooth ripping blade.

A push block and feather board keeps downward pressure on the table and against the fence for the rip cut. Push the work piece well past the blade at the end of the cut.

The first cut complete. Cut the outside face off the remaining legs.

The fence and feather board will need to be readjusted for the remaining cuts. The jointed and mortised sides of the legs are placed against the table top and the fence for the final two cuts. The push block keeps your hands safely out of the way.

The final pass.

With two cuts complete, the leg is rotated end for end to make the final pass. This is the view from the operator's side of the table saw.

The five sided leg. With this first one complete, cut the remaining legs the same way.

Left: Having an extra leg allows me the luxury of setting aside the one with the least appealing grain.

Below: After choosing the four legs with the straightest grain, I place the inside corners together and draw a cabinetmakers triangle on the tops. This helps me identify one leg from another quickly. I also mark each leg with initials such as RF for right front and so on.

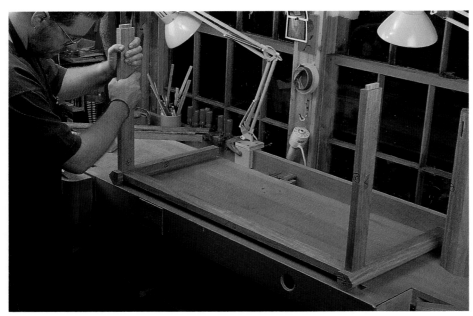

Using short test tenons, the frame is assembled for the first time.

The assembled frame.

While working on the frame pieces for this table, I've been imagining a wood to complement the red/gold color of the narra. Choosing the right color for the top can enhance the table's already warm tone. After sorting through a number of planks, I came across this piece of machiche, wood from Central America , with a rich color that may go nicely with the narra. It also has a very different texture which I feel will complement the frame. The plank's surface was fairly smooth, but using a cabinet scraper to refine it further gives me an idea of what the texture and color will really be like.

I apply a small amount of naphtha to both woods to get an idea of what the colors will be like later when a finish is applied. Naphtha is a mild solvent used to remove wax. It evaporates after about a minute. Use naphtha in a well ventilated area.

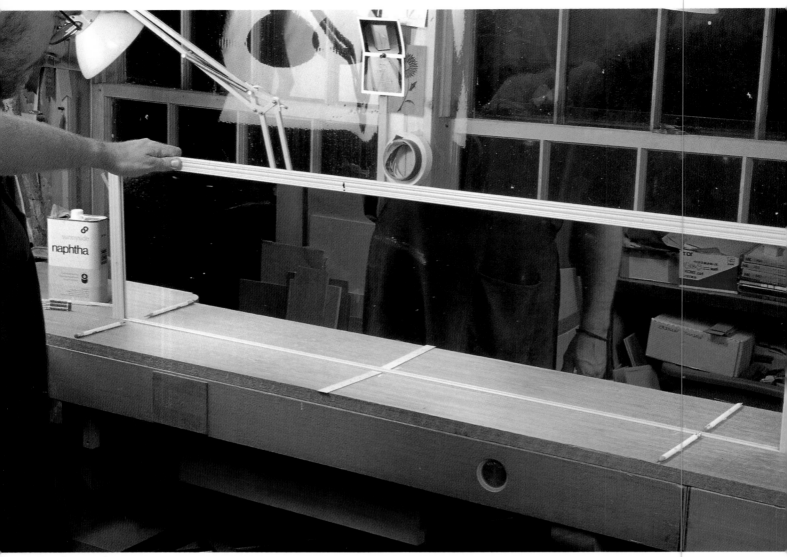

The table top will be made of sawn veneers glued to a plywood core and edge banded with wide pieces of narra. This veneered panel works very well in this application, because it is very stable. This is important because the top sets down within the top of the legs. If a solid wood top were be used in this application, seasonal expansion of the top across the grain would put pressure on the tops of the legs, eventually forcing the joinery apart or buckling the top. Another attractive benefit of sawing the plank into veneers is much greater yield out of the plank. This plank measures 1" by 6" by 96". By resawing it into veneers, I'll have enough materials to cover both the top and the bottom of the top panel with veneers left over. If I were to make the same size top out of solid wood, I would need a second plank to create the same square footage. Not only that, veneering is a lot of fun.

I use a long mirror to better visualize what bookmatched or mirror-imaged combinations of the plank will look like. By flipping the board around and looking at bookmatches from various locations, I determine which section of the plank will provide the most attractive pattern. Two 22" sections have been mapped out with pencils and a ruler that have the most interesting and attractive grain pattern. They happen to fall in the middle of the plank. Both ends of the plank are long enough to also be cut into veneers and used on the bottom side of the table. Their grain is slightly slashed and makes a less attractive series of bookmatches. A second wood species could also be used for the bottom side.

When combining woods on the same plywood core, it's a good idea to choose a wood of similar density so that one side of the plywood panel doesn't pull or have a tendency to warp more so than the other. Similarly, dense woods tend to counter each other. I'm running the grain of this table top across the width, rather than with the length, requiring veneers that are around 22" long, about 3" longer than the top panel is wide. The extra length gives me the option of later adjusting the sawn veneers to line up the bookmatch pattern.

Above: I mark off the 22" sections of the plank with a square and cross cut on the table saw. The shorter length will be easier to joint, wasting less material.

Right: Draw slash lines on the edge of each piece that represents the grain direction. This tells which way the board is to be passed over the jointer. If the grain direction is difficult to see, take a light pass on the edge to clean up the surface.

Draw a series of reference lines along the surface of each board to be jointed. This helps tell when the entire surface has been contacted by the jointer cutters and is flat.

Joint each of the boards. Notice the grain direction slash mark drawn on the edge in the photograph.

On the end of each board, draw a cabinetmaker's triangle. This will aid in reassembling the veneers once they're sliced off. If the triangle varies a little bit from board to board, it also helps to identify which veneers came from which original board.

Set up the bandsaw as done previously when milling up the rough lumber. When sawing veneers it is very important to set the drift accurately and adjust the thrust bearings and guide blocks at the bandsaw. Also check that the fence is parallel with the blade for uniform cuts.

I use the same 1/2" blade with four hook teeth per inch as used earlier. This blade is bi-metal, which lasts longer than high carbon blades. It's time well spent to properly set up the saw. The resulting veneers will be consistent and satisfying. Set the fence approximately 3/32" from the blade. Clamp at the front and back of the fence and cut a small test piece. Adjust the fence if the result is much over or under 3/32".

Use a steady feed rate when sawing the veneers. Pushing the work piece too fast often results in an uneven cut, as the blade has the tendency to wander. If you push too slow, the blade may burn the wood. Do it just right and you have a perfect veneer. I try to position my hand so I don't need to regrip the work piece in mid-cut, which often causes a bump in the veneer. After each of the veneers is sawn off, the board can be lightly rejointed to true up the surface. Often, I skip this step if all is going well. The surface created by the bandsaw blade is consistent and the board usually remains flat after each pass. Depending on the thickness of the original board, I sometimes get an extra veneer by not jointing between passes. This board measured around 3/4" after initial jointing and I estimate that it would be a stretch to get five veneers. So I lightly jointed after each veneer was sawn.

The resulting stack of sawn veneers.

Left: The veneers can then be sent through a drum sander or thickness planer to smooth the surface and level any high spots. I prefer the drum sander since it leaves virtually no snipe. Two passes with 150 grit sandpaper is usually all that is required. The final thickness is a strong 1/16".

Below: The cabinetmakers triangle helps assemble the veneers in the order in which they grew, an important consideration when bookmatching.

Right: Separating the reassembled stack as shown is one possibility for creating a balanced pattern. This is a chance to experiment with different combinations of matching veneers to arrive at an attractive overall pattern.

Below: This is the arrangement I've decided on. A cabinetmakers triangle that crosses each of the veneers will help to reassemble the pattern through the following steps.

SHOOTING VENEERS

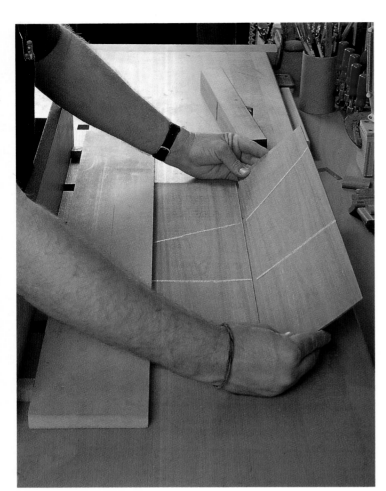

Left: The veneers need to be edge joined together in pairs, until a continuous sheet is created. The joint between each pair of veneers needs to be "shot" or edge jointed with a long jointer plane. This technique will leave a perfect edge to edge joint with an invisible seam. Start by folding the pair of veneers together.

Below left: Place the veneers on a long piece of MDF (medium density fiber board) with the edges to be joined hanging over slightly.

Below right: Position a second piece of MDF over the veneers. Use the sole of the plane to tap the veneers until they are perfectly flush with each other.

Left: One hand holds the top piece of MDF firmly on the veneers, while the other hand slides the jointer plane, which is laying on its side, along the edge of the two veneers. Two or three passes with the plane is often enough to create a perfect joint. Sandpaper glued to the bottom of the lower piece of MDF helps hold the assembly in place on the bench. By planing the two veneers at the same time, even if the plane's side is not square to the sole, the joint will still fit since any out of true jointing angle is transferred to both veneers.

Below: Open up the veneers and press the seam together to check for a perfect fit. If the joint can be pressed together easily with hand pressure, the pair is ready to glue together. If any gaps are visible, repeat the process until the joint is perfect.

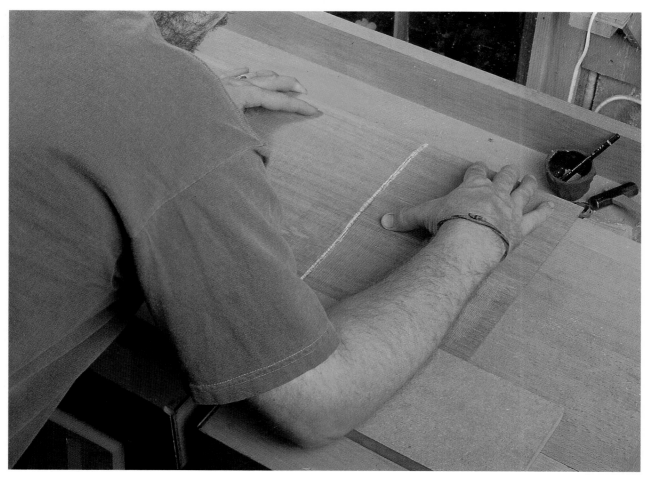

EDGE GLUING THE VENEERS

Above: This is the arrangement I use for edge gluing the veneers. The set up consists of a large piece of MDF placed on saw horses as a temporary table. Newspaper prevents the veneers from becoming glued to the MDF. A straight piece of wood is clamped along both edges of the MDF to serve as stationary fences. The spacing between the strips is about 3/4" wider than the width of a pair of veneers. Low angle wooden wedges used in pairs apply pressure to the joint while the glue dries. The wedges are about 1/2" thick and were sawn on the bandsaw. Strips of newspaper are placed below the seam.

Left: Use an accordion glue bottle to apply a nice bead of yellow woodworker's glue to one of the edges. The pinky finger helps to guide the tip of the glue bottle.

Place the veneer back on the table and press the two veneers together. Pair up the wedges using hand pressure to force the joint tight. If too much pressure is applied, the veneers will buckle.

Feeling through the glue, tap the joint flush if necessary.

Place more newspaper strips over the glue joint and lay a heavy flat piece of wood on top to weigh the veneers down. Tap the wedges slightly with a hammer to increase pressure. After 30 minutes the assembly can be taken apart and the next pair can be glued. The completed pair will still be fragile for a while, so handle with care. Hang the glued veneers on something like a clothesline or lay them on a flat surface and weight down to prevent the pair from cupping.

After all the pairs are glued together, they can be glued into double pairs and so on until the length of the table top is achieved. As the sheet of veneer grows larger than the glue up table, one portion of the sheet can hang off the table with one of the straight wooden pieces that makes the stationary fence clamped on top of it. The process gets repeated to make up the veneer sheet that will become the bottom side of the table top.

Above: Once all the veneer pairs have been edge glued together to form a sheet, I set them aside to dry for a few hours so they can be handled more easily. Careful work has resulted in seams that are nearly flat and only require a small amount of work to level out. The surfaces need to be leveled to assure good glue bond with the plywood core. This can be done with a cabinet scraper at the bench or with a drum sander. I've found it best to level both the glue side and the face side at this time, minimizing the amount of work after the veneer has been glued to the core.

Left: The width of the veneer sheet is wider than the capacity of the sander. The amount of leveling I am doing is minimal so the center area can be worked on at the bench.

TOP PANEL GLUE-UP PREPARATION

Left: Once both top and bottom veneers have been leveled, the plywood core and the veneers can be cut to the same size. I've chosen 1/2" Baltic birch plywood for the core. Orienting the sheet so that the face grain of the plywood runs perpendicular to the grain of the veneer. Rip all the material to a dimension 1" longer and wider than the final size.

Below left: Cut the veneer sheets to width. Using the same fence set up, also cut a piece of 1/8" or 1/4" masonite or lunan plywood at the same time, to be used as a caul in the vacuum press.

Below right: Cross cut a square edge on the veneers, plywood core, and the caul material.

Above: Cross cut all pieces to final over size length.

Left: With the parts cut that will make up the top panel, preparation can be made for the glue up. I like to provide a means of locating the veneers to the core so that they don't slide around after glue has been applied, making positioning difficult. The top veneer is carefully lined up with the plywood core and clamped together. A small dowel can be used as a locator. I use bamboo 1skewers, however an 1/8" dowel would work as well.

Drill a hole located about 1/2" from the end of the board, which the bamboo skewer will fit snuggly into. This hole is drilled about 1/4" deep. This places the locating pin in an area that will later be cut off. I use a story stick which represents the exact final length of the top panel to double check that I'm drilling beyond the required length.

Above left: Cut a few short lengths of skewer that will act as pins. Here I use a small cut off box with a fine-toothed saw.

Above right: Tap a skewer pin into place and pare the pin flush with a chisel. Repeat the process at the other end of the panel, being sure to drill outside the final dimension of

the top. Having located this side of the top, flip the panel upside down and repeat at both ends of the bottom veneer. Be careful not to drill into the previous skewer on the other side of the panel. I draw a cabinetmakers triangle on the edge of the temporarily assembled top so I don't try to locate a veneer in the wrong place after glue is applied .

Glue up top. I find it best to do a dry run for the glue up. This will assure that all the required tools and supplies are laid out and within arm's reach. Prepare the vacuum bag by unrolling it on a bench or table, on top of a sheet or blanket to protect the bottom of the bag. A platen made of 3/4" MDF (medium density fiberboard) or plywood goes inside the bag. The platen has a grid of 1/8" deep grooves cut on both sides to aid in evacuating air from the bag.

The airline that connects the bag with the vacuum

pump is inserted through the bag and into the platen. Within reach is the bag's clamping device which is a plastic tube and plastic c-channel that squeezes the bag around the tube for an air tight seal. Also within reach is a piece of plastic sheet that measures a little larger than the top panel. The plastic sheet is wrapped around the panel before the assembly is placed in bag. This keeps glue off the inside of the bag. Apply painters masking tape to the face of one of the veneers to speed up the positioning of the panel after glue has been applied.

Left: I'm using yellow woodworkers glue for the adhesive. It's appropriate and convenient for this glue up. Its downside is that it has a short working time before it grabs. I want to have the panel in the vacuum bag before that happens, otherwise there's a risk of the veneer not bonding to the core. If I needed more working time I could choose white woodworkers glue, or a plastic resin glue that requires mixing.

The glue can be applied with a notched trowel or a small foam roller. Both do a nice job of evenly spreading the adhesive. Turn the veneer face down and place the core on top of it. Apply a consistent amount to the one side of the core. If glue is applied to the veneer instead, the veneer will cup, making assembly difficult. The vacuum bag has a tendency to draw glue into the wood of both the plywood and veneer, so I apply a little more than I would if I were using a conventional veneer press or clamps. Roll on additional glue to areas that seem dry.

Below left: Flip the plywood glue side down on top of the taped veneer using the locating pins to align the two. Apply approximately the same amount of glue to the new side of the plywood.

Below right: Position the second veneer over the glued plywood lining up the locating pins. Stretch the tape from the bottom veneer and wrap around the top.

Place the pre-cut caul on top of the assembly and tape around the package. The edges of the caul have been rounded over to protect the vacuum bag from sharp edges. The assembled package is placed on top of the sheet of plastic, which is wrapped around all four sides and is quickly taped in place.

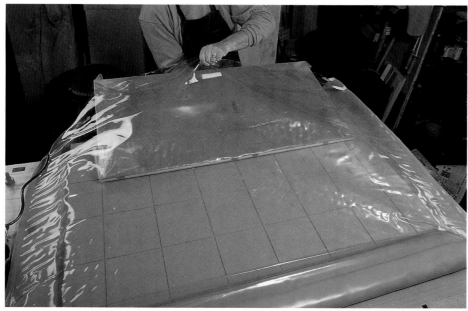

This whole assembly is then slid into the bag and roughly centered on the platen. The bag's clamping device, which is the plastic pipe with the plastic c-channel, is used to enclose the bag.

With the closure tightly sealing the open end of the bag the vacuum pump is turned on. On a flat panel such as this, it takes less than 60 seconds for the vacuum pump to evacuate the air from the bag. As this is happening I keep my hands moving around the surface flatting out the vinyl bag and keeping it pressed tightly up against the work piece.

One of the real benefits of using a vacuum bag is that it applies even pressure to the entire surface of the panel which can be difficult with mechanical clamps. Once the air has been evacuated from the bag I look to see that I'm getting even glue squeezed out around all four edges of the panel. This will show up as small dots of glue if I've put on the appropriate amount. Sometimes a flashlight is handy to see the edges. I'll leave the panel in the bag for three or four hours. Once the panel is taken out of the bag I'll scrape off any excess glue and sandwich the panel between two thick pieces of flat plywood and clamp them in place. This will allow the panel to cure and remain flat.

The panel has set for a couple of days after coming out of the vacuum bag. The precaution of having consistently thick veneers on each side of the panel, allowing the panel to dry flat, and choosing high quality flat plywood to begin with have resulted in a nice, flat panel. Clamped to the bench, a block plane is used to initially straighten the edge and remove dried glue.

A wooden smoothing plane with a 90 degree fence attached to its sole is used to flatten and square the edges. Sighting down the sole from behind allows me to watch for a glint of steel emerging as the iron is lightly tapped with a hammer. Tap the iron left or right as needed to adjust the cutting edge parallel with the sole.

Draw a series of reference lines on the edge as reference marks for hand-jointing the edge.

The first couple of passes will give you an idea of the high spots on the edge. When using a hand plane, pressure is applied to the front of the plane at the beginning of the cut. In the middle of the cut, pressure is even on the front and back of the plane. As the plane approaches the end of the panel the hand pressure shifts to the back of the plane. This helps in creating a perfectly straight edge. Apply consistent pressure on the side of the plane to keep the fence against the panel.

Use a straight edge to check the panel edge. Sight underneath the straight edge for any hint of light, telling whether the edge is high in the middle or on the ends. If no light is visible, the edge is perfectly straight.

Use a small 90 degree square to double check that the edge has also been planed square to the face.

With the long edge planed straight and square rotate the work piece to work on the short edge of the table top. Clamped in position repeat the process of drawing reference lines and planing them away until the edge is straight and square.

Above: Check with an accurate square, the relationship of the long edge to the freshly jointed short edge. If this is perfectly square, it's time to move onto the next step. If not, make minor adjustments and continue until it is square. Accurate work at this stage will make the project easier when fitting the top to the frame. If the hand plane is not cutting well, check the iron's sharpness.

Left: A pair of story sticks have been made to represent the plywood panel's length and width. These dimensions are the exact length of the long and short rails of the frame. Using the story stick that represents the width, adjust the table saw's fence so that the distance between the fence and the blade is a tiny bit longer than the story stick (approximately 1/32"). Clamp the fence into position.

Left: With the recently jointed long edge of the panel against the table saw's fence, rip the panel to width. Applying a long strip of masking tape to the bottom side of the panel will decrease the risk of the table saw blade splintering out the bottom side. Once the width is cut, repeat the previous two steps with the length of the panel. The end result is a panel that is approximately 1/32" too long and too wide to fit within the legs of the frame. The final fit is achieved with a hand plane back at the bench.

Below left: With the panel clamped securely in the bench and working on the long edge, use the 90 degree smoothing plane to clean up the table saw marks and establish a second perfectly straight and parallel long edge. The story stick is held flush against one edge and gives a reading at the opposite edge of how much material needs to be planed away. Once the story stick and the width of the panel are identical the long edge is finished. Repeat the process for the short edge, again using the story stick for a point of reference.

Below right: All four edges of the plywood have been accurately planed square, straight, and parallel to each other. To double check this take a diagonal measurement from corner to corner to make sure the distance is identical. The final check is to see that the panel fits within the dry clamped frame, both in its length and its width. It should be a friction fit.

With the plywood panel complete it's time to make the edge bandings. These edge bandings were milled oversized when the rest of the lumber was sawn and jointed. Set the bandsaw fence approximately 1" from the blade. With the previously jointed face and edge against the bandsaw table and fence, resaw the edge stock to a rough dimension of approximately 1" by 1 1/2".

Run all four pieces through the thickness planer, making sure to plane with the grain. Plane the edge bandings to about 7/8" thick and 1 3/8" wide.

The edge banding pieces are going to be joined to the top with a spline. The spline will be 1/4" wide and the spline groove will be approximately 1/2" deep. This 1/4" three winged slot cutter has a radiused edge on each of the carbide cutters. This radiused edge is used for some other specialty shop functions and will not be a factor for this spline groove. The distance between the end of the cutter and the guide bearing is 1/2".

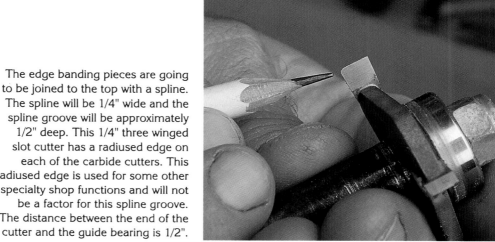

The router is adjusted so that the cutter creates a groove in the center of the edge of the long and short edge banding pieces. Repeat this router pass for all four edge banding pieces. I try to make the groove in two or three shallow passes.

Resaw some remaining narra stock to make the spline. The rough dimension of this stock will be 3/8" by 1 1/8". Once the narra is resawn, run the spline stock through the thickness planer until it measures just under 1" wide and 1/4" thick.

A groove made by the same slot cutter has been routed in the edge of a scrap piece of plywood. This scrape becomes a gauge to determine the final thickness of the spline. Once the spline fits snuggly in the spline groove the thickness planing is complete.

Moving onto the top panel, the process of routing the groove is repeated. The edge banding stock has been milled so that it is thicker than the top panel by about 1/8". This takes the worry out of gluing the edge banding precisely flush with the top panel. By being proud of the surface on both sides of the top panel, I have the luxury of planing, scraping or sanding the surfaces flush after the glue up has dried. Rather than reset the router bit depth, I prefer to shim the router with a thin scrap, in this case a piece of commercial veneer. Shimming the router offsets the groove by the thickness of the shim. When the spline and the edge band are assembled the edge band will set above the top panel the thickness of the veneer shim. The clamps are placed so that they don't interfere with the router.

Rout the top panel by moving the router left to right . Make two or three passes to reach the full depth.

Left: Test fit the spline and edge banding together. The edge banding should be proud of both the top and bottom of the panel. Hand pressure should be enough to eliminate any space between the edge banding and the top panel.

Below: To provide a space for excess glue, chamfer the sharp corners of the spline. A small trimming plane or block plane works well.

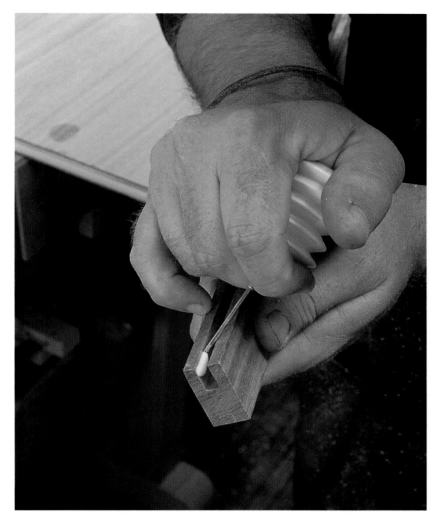

Left: Edge band glue up. Pipe clamps, spaced about 6" apart, apply pressure on the splined edge bandings. Set the clamps up on a bench or table top ahead of time and go through a dry run to make sure the clamps are positioned correctly. Shim the panel with plywood scraps in order to elevate the work piece so the center of the panel lines up with the center of the clamp screw. This helps prevent the top panel from bowing up or down under pressure, possibly creating a gap between the edge and the top.

Apply yellow glue to the long grooves of both panels and edge band. A small accordion glue bottle works well. The long edge bandings are still longer than the panel and will be trimmed later. Make sure the ends of both edge banding pieces stick out at both ends. After assembling everything by hand, tighten the clamps. Medium clamp pressure will draw the edges tight. Check that the seam is tight along its entire length. Allow to dry three or four hours.

Below: For photography purposes, I'm continuing the process on another table. This table is identical to the narra table in dimensions, and is made of black walnut with red gum for the veneered top panel. Once removed from the clamps, the panel is ready for the next glue up. Notice the edge bandings are slightly longer than the top. The blue tape aids in making sure the different pieces are glued in place right side up.

Above: Applied edge bandings, proud of the table top surface.

Left: With the top panel held vertically in a bench vise, apply two layers of masking tape to the plywood edge against the edge banding. This will serve as a shim for trimming off the edge banding.

Below: I saw with little or no "set" works well for trimming the edge banding nearly flush. Keep pressure with a finger flat on the masking tape and carefully saw the edge banding.

Above: A fast cutting woodworking file is used to sneak up on a perfectly flush edge. Draw pencil reference lines on the plywood edge to prevent over-filing. Tape wrapped around the front end of the file can help prevent the file from damaging the edge of the veneer panel. File from the outside of the edge toward the panel to prevent splintering. Stop when the pencil lines first begin to disappear and the two pieces feel flush.

Right: Check with a straight edge. When perfect, repeat the process on the remaining three corners.

The short edge bandings need to be cut to their final length before they're glued in place. Clamp square blocks of scrap to the ends of one long edge banding as shown. These provide a solid stop for determining the exact length of the edge banding. Notice the 1/4" masonite shims beneath the panel, elevating the top to line up with the center line of the clamps.

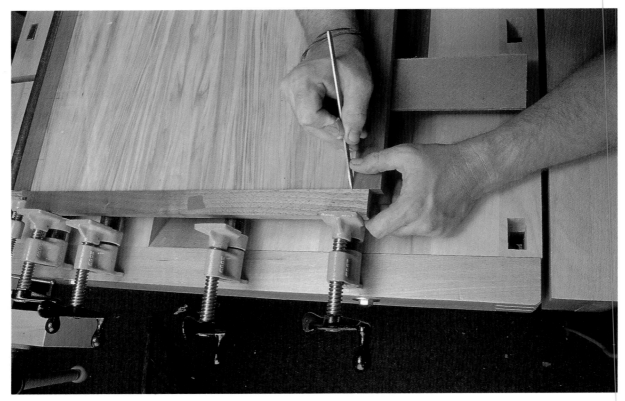

With one end of the edge banding cut square and butted up against the clamped stop block, mark the end of the veneer panel with a marking knife. Repeat the process at the other end of the top. Cut the banding edge pieces just longer than this mark and shoot the ends square to the knife mark on the shooting board. Double check that the length is perfect.

Apply glue to the edge bandings and veneered top panel. Insert spline and press into place. Be sure to butt the edge banding against the clamped stop block before clamping. Work quickly and reposition the edge banding if necessary. I find it helpful to start applying pressure with the clamp farthest from the clamp block. This tends to squeeze the edge banding towards the stop block. A flashlight is helpful for checking the fit of the edge banding and panel.

Applied edge banding approximately
centered height wise in the clamps.

After the edge bandings have dried, a smoothing plane and cabinet scraper will quickly
bring the proud edge bandings flush with the veneer. I like to set up two smoothing
planes, one set fairly coarse to remove most of the oversized edge and another set very
fine to make the final few passes. The walnut edge banding on this top planed well with
the exception of a couple of spots where the grain changed directions. These areas were
leveled with a small cabinet scraper working at an angle to the edge.

Although care has been taken in choosing flat plywood and consistently thin veneers, the top panel is seldom perfectly flat at this stage. A finely tuned cabinet scraper will level the surface very efficiently. This wooden cabinet scraper is about 9" long with a 1 3/4" blade. The tool is used much like a smoothing plane. Pressure is applied to the front of the scraper at the beginning of the stroke. The pressure shifts to the middle of the scraper through the middle of the stroke and moves to the back of the body at the end of the stroke. Care is needed at the end of the stroke to prevent the blade from digging in and damaging the surface as it exits the board. Work diagonally across the panel, then diagonally in the opposite direction. Finally, long strokes along the length.

The process is repeated until the scraper is taking shavings over the entire surface. By this time, the scraper may be in need of a fresh burr, just as with the hand scraper described previously. With the cabinet scraper carefully adjusted to take a very fine shaving, one final round of passes across the entire surface completes the leveling. The surface can than be refined with a sharp hand scraper. The hand scraper will remove any marks left by the cabinet scraper. For most woods, several rounds of sanding can be eliminated by scraping the surface. Any sanding that needs to be done is with only the finer grits.

The top is finished off by hand sanding, using a long cork faced block. This one is sized for half sheets of sand paper. Start with 220 grit paper being careful to sand with the grain of the veneer and avoid rounding the ends. Work across the surface until all imperfections from the previous steps are removed and the surface texture is consistent. Brush off the dust and repeat with 320 grit, then 400 grit. The raw surface will have a soft sheen.

Above: Cross grained sanding marks at the two ends can be removed with a sharp scraper and a light touch.

Right: A carefully sharpened scraper will produce shavings on most woods. If scraping results in dust, it's time to try another edge or lay a new burr.

Left: An alternative to scraping is the use of an orbital palm sander. Since the sander does not span a long distance like a scraper plane or sanding block, care must be taken to avoid making subtle dips across the surface. By working in a variety of patterns, such as long overlapping passes and circular motions and by keeping the sander moving it does a nice job. I've progressed from 100 grit to 220 grit eliminating marks from the previous round before moving on to the next finer grit. Even with the high quality of the recent generation of sanders, careful observation with good light will often reveal tiny sanding marks. I choose to remove these by hand with a sanding block as before. Start with 220 grit and work up to 400 grit.

Below left: Reference marks in pencil help in the leveling process.

Below right: Having completed the top and bottom surfaces of the top panel, work can begin on the edges. For supporting a large panel vertically over the side of the bench, I use shop-made fixtures that fit into the bench dog holes. They are appropriately named "bench puppies."

The bench puppies hold the work securely, allowing full length plane passes. A plane with a 90 degree edge fence set for a fairly heavy cut removes material quickly. Here, I eventually remove about 1/8" of wood. Check the process by setting the top panel in place on the dry clamped frame. I plane the edges until it lines up with the sides of the 45 degree legs.

When the edge in nearly finished, I switch to another smoothing plane, which is set for a very fine cut. Two or three shavings later I have a perfectly smooth, crisp edge.

A small trimming plane takes down the sharp edges. It can be slightly rounded or chamfered. Repeat the process for the remaining edges. With this complete, the top can be safely set aside while the frame is completed.

Test fitting the top in place on the frame can help locate any edges that need further attention as well as checking the fit of the edge bandings between the legs.

Above: Shaping the legs. A simple leg holding jig can be made from the triangular scraps left over from cutting the 45 degree angles off the legs. Glue a pair of triangular scraps side by side to a couple of pieces of small plywood and allow to dry for twenty minutes.

Right: Before clamping the leg in the bench, pencil on the grain direction on the different faces of the leg. This tells you at a glance what direction to plane.

I start with the outer face of the leg placing the 45 degree inside corner down on the leg holding jig and clamping it between the bench dogs.

A smoothing plane set for a fairly heavy cut quickly shapes the round face of the leg. Work until the curve is consistent across the face of the leg. Once shaped, adjust the plane for a finer cut and work the curve surface until it's nicely shaped.

Left: Rotate the leg to one of the flat faces, again checking for grain direction before planing. The V-shaped leg holding jigs can be placed aside for now. Two or three light passes will true the flat surfaces, removing the saw marks and smoothing the surface.

Below: The finish left by a sharp hand plane brings out a rich luster in the wood. Continue planing all the flat surfaces including the two faces with the mortises.

Left: The sharp inside corner of the leg (the corner that faces the center of the table) can be eased with a tapered chamfer. This means taking more material off at the bottom of the leg and almost none at the top. This can be done with a small plane. I use a Japanese chamfer plane for this step, mainly because I like the plane. It also happens to do a nice job.

Start by taking a short chamfer pass (2" long or so) at the foot of the leg. Then take a 4" pass followed by a 6" pass and so on. Don't plane at all at the top couple of inches of the leg. Begin the process again at the bottom, this essentially removes more material at the bottom than at the top and is an excellent way to quickly taper something using a hand plane.

Below left: Back to the curved face, using a very thin hand scraper that will flex to the curve of the leg. Work the surface, smoothing the tiny ridges left by the smoothing plane. This thin scraper was made from a worn out Japanese saw blade, with the teeth filed off and prepared as any other scraper. The flexibility and high quality of the steel is perfect for a scraper.

Below right: A cabinet scraper replaces the hand plane when working with roed wood such as narra. The cabinet scraper works beautifully for creating the curved face as well as smoothing the flat faces.

A thin flexible hand scraper refines the curve. Once scraping is complete, the surfaces can be sanded with sandpaper and a sanding block. Start with 220 grit sandpaper and work up through 400 grit. A thick piece of foam placed between the sanding block and sandpaper will help the paper conform to the curved face. Neoprene from an old wet suit works well.

Clamp the leg with the foot up and file the bevel along the edges. This visually separates the table leg from the floor it will sit on.

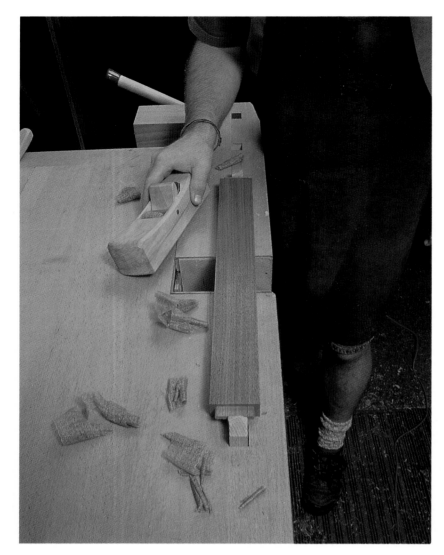

The rails can now be hand finished with hand planes or scrapers and sandpaper, depending on the wood. Smooth all four surfaces removing any joiner or saw marks. Spline tenons, dry fit into the rail mortises, protect the rails from the pressure of the bench dogs.

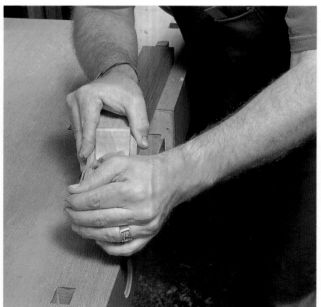

The size of the rails are good for practicing the plane stroke.

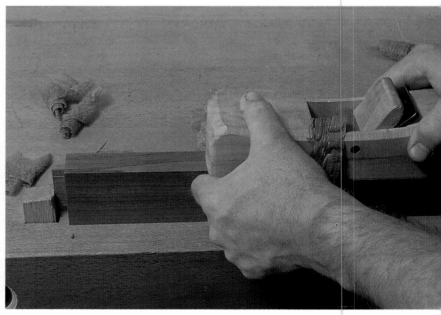

Planing the edge of the rails.

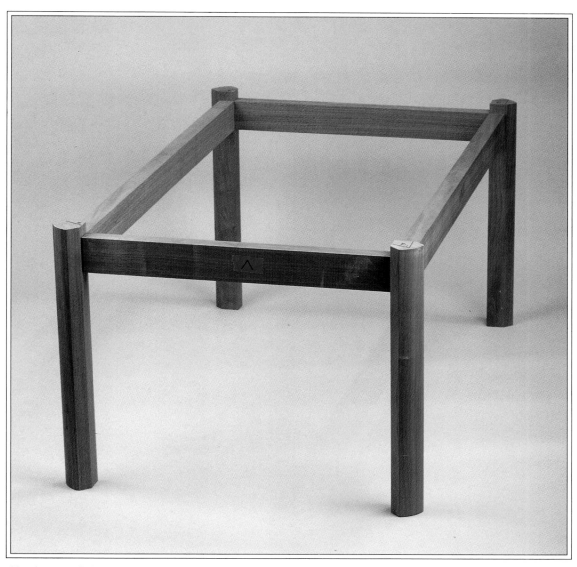

Here's a good chance to dry assemble the table frame and see how it looks. This is an opportunity to make subtle changes with a hand plane, files, etc. Sometimes straight legs can look visually wider at the bottom and some tapering may be in order to correct this illusion.

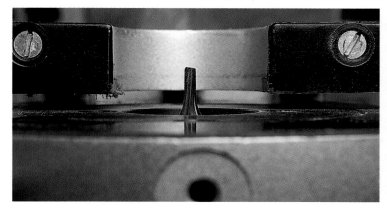

Above: Next I rout a small cove shape along the top outside edge of each rail piece. Since the top overhangs the rail by only a small amount, I feel this cove helps to visually separate the two when the table is viewed from a low angle. The cove shows up as a dark line just below the top panel. I use a single edge 1/8" router bit that has had the corner rounded over slightly with a file. This makes a pleasantly shaped cove.

Right: With the rails positioned right side up, clamp in place, set the router fence, and take a shallow pass.

A small piece of 320 grit sandpaper wrapped around a small scrap of wood smoothes the routed cove.

Ease the sharp edges all around each rail.

The spline tenons can be glued into the rails at this point. Double check that the loose tenons can be pushed into the mortises by hand. Remove the tenon and apply glue around the upper half of the mortise. Spread the glue around evenly. An accordion glue bottle works well for this.

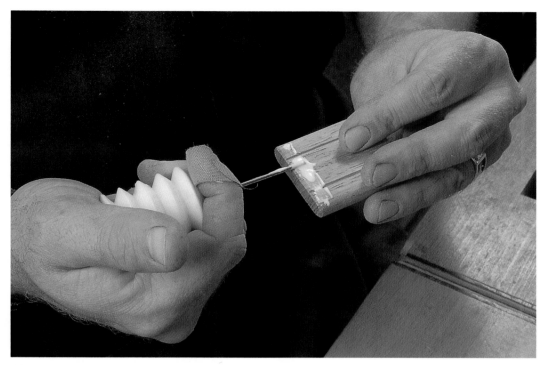

Also, apply glue around one end of the spline tenon. When inserted, the tenon will move glue into the depth of the mortise.

Push the tenon in place.
Tap home if necessary.

A small artist spatula easily cleans up squeeze out before it dries.

MITERED TENONS

Once the glue has dried, the end of each tenon needs to be trimmed off at a 45 degree angle. This will allow a long rail tenon and a short rail tenon to fit properly in each leg mortises. The tenon is trimmed off on the table saw with the blade tilted to 45 degrees. With one of the long rails face up on the saw, use the saw's miter gauge to cut a miter on the tenon. The blade is tilted away from the workpiece. Compare the length of the mitered tenon with the depth of the mortise. Aim at having the tenon about 1/64" shorter than the mortise is deep.

When you are satisfied with the tenon's length, make a mark on the miter gauge fence that locates the shoulder of the rail. The remaining cuts can be lined up with this rail mark. Rotate the long rail end for end, line up the rail's shoulder with the locating mark, and trim the tenon to length. Make sure to keep the rail face up on the saw. Repeat the cut on both ends of each of the four rails. As a final test of the proper mitered tenon length, dry fit a long and short rail to a leg and make sure that both fit tight against the leg.

Glue up the ends. Make padded clamping blocks as seen. The 45 degree cuts can be made on the bandsaw or table saw.

Go through a dry run with two legs and one short rail clamped together to make sure everything fits tightly.

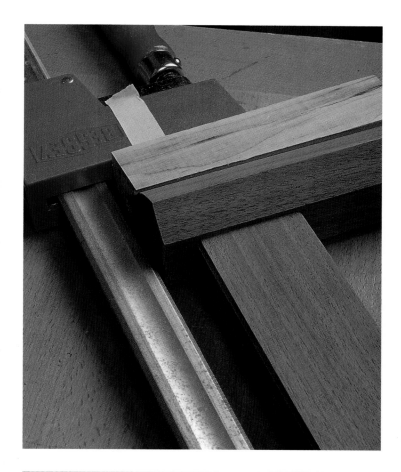

Left: Remove the clamps and apply glue to the correct mortises and tenons as done previously. Make sure that the rail is positioned right side up. Push the rail onto both tenons. Use clamps and clamp pads to squeeze the joints tight. Check the front and back. Adjust the clamps if the joints have not closed up nicely. Repeat for the other legs and short rail. Set aside for three or four hours to dry.

Below left: After the glue up has dried, carefully pare off any glue that has squeezed out with a sharp chisel.

Below right: The tops of each leg can be shaped or "pillowed" with woodworking files or sandpaper. Using the special clamping blocks, clamp one of the legs up right in the bench vise. A cork faced sanding block with 220 grit sandpaper works well in creating a slight dome on top of the leg. Masking tape applied to the top of the rail near the leg, protects the rail from accidental damage from the sandpaper. If 220 grit sandpaper is not effective on denser woods for this initial shaping, 150 grit paper or a fine woodworking file may be more appropriate. NOTE: This step can also be done before the legs are glued to the short rails if you anticipate a problem clamping the partially assembled frame for shaping.

Ease the edges and sand the top of the legs smooth. A few
minutes spent with 220 grit sandpaper will leave a nicely pillowed
top, with the center of the top about 1/16" higher than the edges.
Smooth the shape with 320 grit and 400 grit sandpaper.

The pencil line near the top of the leg and above the rail indicates the top edge of
the veneered top panel. Stay above the line while shaping the leg. This leg can use
a little more pillowing before moving onto the next leg. I like a pillowed surface like
this to be softly rounded without looking mushy. A reckless use of sandpaper or a
power sander when working edges and details can often result in a loss of crispness.

DRY FIT

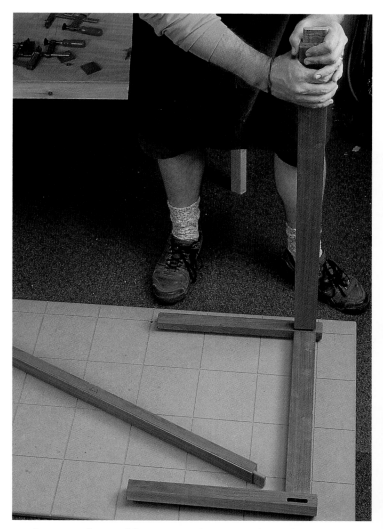

Lay an end assembly mortise side up on a flat surface. Here I use a MDF platen borrowed from the vacuum press. With the dry spline tenons in place, insert the long rails.

Position the opposite end assembly over the spline tenons.

Place the table frame legs down and tap the joint together if needed. Use the 45 degree clamping pad for tapping.

Use rubber bands to hold the clamping pads in place, freeing up your hands to position and adjust the clamps. Here I'm using heavy duty pipe clamps. Notice the blue tape identifying the different rails and how they relate to the legs.

Center the clamps on the joint as much as possible. Beware of having the clamp's black pipe in contact with the table frame. As the clamp is tightened, the pipe will flex, possibly damaging the wood.

With both sides clamped tightly, use a pair of diagonal sticks to check the squareness of the frame. Diagonal sticks are pieces of straight wood that have a long point planed on one end of each. This is a more accurate way of checking a diagonal dimension than a ruler or tape measure. Fit the points of the sticks diagonally between two legs and clamp the sticks together.

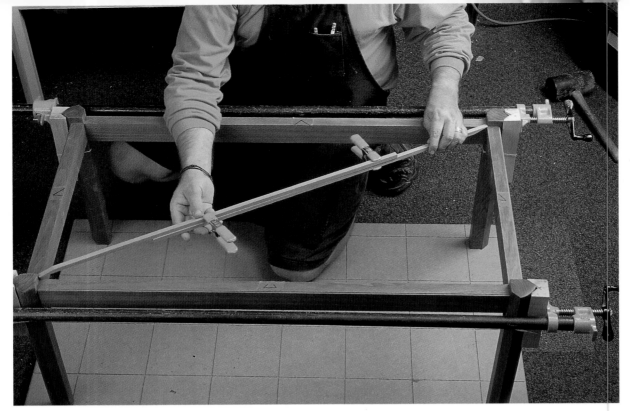

Check the diagonal dimensions between the opposite pair of legs. If the diagonal dimension is not the same both ways, clamps need to be relocated slightly and diagonals checked again. Continue adjusting the clamps until the diagonal dimensions are the same. We know that the rail lengths are identical, so any out of squareness is the result of skewed clamp pressure.

Because of the short reach of the pipe clamp heads and the distance the angled legs stick out beyond the rail, I've decided to approach the clamping with a pair of pipe clamps on each side. The first clamp will hang over the top of the legs, while the second clamp will reach from inside the legs below the end rails. Tape small pieces of cardboard to the top of each leg to protect them from the clamps. This clamp arrangement has proved better for getting the pressure close to the center of the joint. These decisions are a lot less stressful now, going through the dry run, rather than later with glue on the joinery.

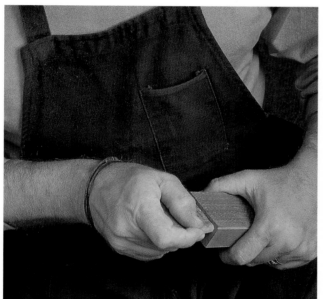

Above: Glue spline tenons to the rails, applying glue around the top half of the mortise and the entry end of the tenon. An artist spatula works well for spreading glue around.

Left: Push tenons into the mortise.

Below: Tap the tenon until it bottoms out in the mortise. Repeat on the remaining rail mortises.

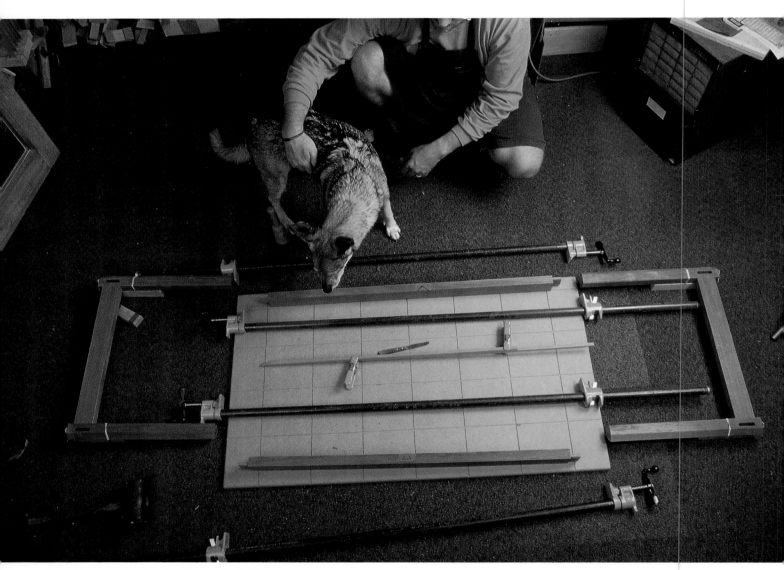

Everything needed for the glue up including
Sidney the "wonder dog" and glue up helper.

Applying glue to the four mortises. I use an accordion glue bottle to coat the glue around the top half of the mortise. When the tenon is inserted, glue will be distributed to the bottom of the mortise.

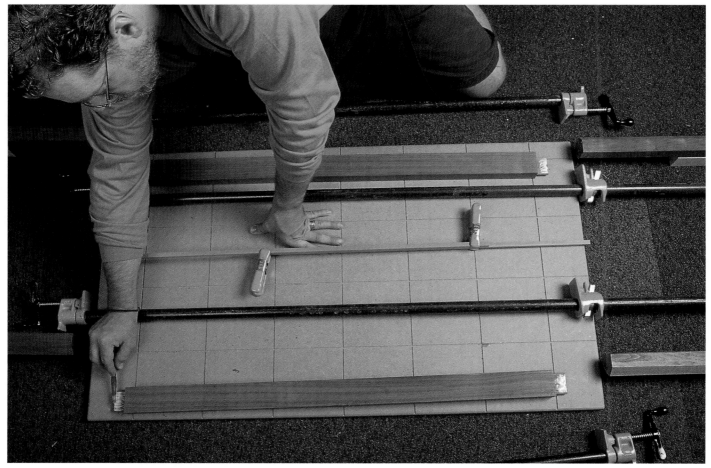

Working quickly, spread glue around the tenons.

137

Left: Assemble the table frame. Push the joints together as much as possible by hand.

Below left: Depending on your level of stress at the moment, tap or pound the the joints closer together. When the joint is close enough, set the table down and start adding the clamps.

Below right: Put the upper clamps on first, since they will support themselves on top of the legs. Tighten the top clamps enough to hold them in place. Position the lower clamps, being careful not to contact the frame with the clamps. Alternate pressure on the upper and lower clamps until the joinery is tight.

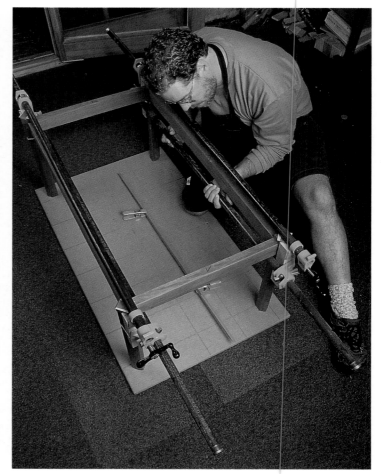

Check diagonals using the diagonal sticks. It's common to need
to release a couple of clamps and slide them one way or
another until the pressure they exert squares up the frame.

Once the diagonal dimension is the same, visually check that all of the joints
are tight using a flashlight. There will likely be small areas of glue squeezing out
of the joints. I like to wait about 15 minutes for the squeeze out to turn rubbery
before removing it. A sharp bamboo skewer works well for getting into tight
corners without smearing the glue or damaging the wood. At this point, I like to
set the clamped frame on a very flat surface like a table saw top while it dries
over night. Once dry, pare off any remaining traces of glue with a sharp chisel.

Left: Next, a means of attaching the top to the base needs to be made. Since we're using a stable veneered top panel, we don't need to allow for top panel movement. Dowels will provide a good junction between the top and the frame. I start by laying out pencil marks about 2" from the end of the rail and then approximately every 4" down the length of the rail. With a shop made pencil gauge, set at half the thickness of the rail, draw cross marks at each of these layout marks.

Below left: Use an awl to start a hole for a brad point drill bit.

Below right: Make a wood drill stop for drilling to a consistent depth. Start with a small square of scrap wood, a couple of inches long. Use a drill press and the same 1/4" brad point drill bit that will be used for the doweling to drill completely through the scrap. Whittle away much of the stop, roughly rounding it. Slide the stop on to the drill bit and up to the chuck. A mark can be made on the stop for the depth of the holes and the stop can be cut off to its final length. The amount of bit protruding through the stop determines its depth.

Left: Drill vertically until the drill contacts the rail surface.

Below left: Use a small countersink to relieve the edge of the hole. This provides a small area for excess glue to gather.

Below right: Use 1/4" dowel centers to transfer the dowel locations to the table top. Put the top in place and press down on the dowel centers to transfer the mark. Repeat until all dowel locations have been transferred.

Moving on to the table top, a washer acts as a spacer to change the drill depth and avoid drilling through the top.

Drill the 1/4" holes in the bottom side of the table top.

Here I use a small cut off box to cut the dowels to length. Combine the depth of a frame hole with that of a top panel hole, less 1/16" for any glue build up, to arrive at the total length of the dowel. Clamp a stop block to the cut off box.

Left: Cut off enough dowels to this length.

Below left: Tap the dowels through a dowel reamer if they fit too tightly in the dowel holes. Use a file to ease the end of the dowels.

Below right: After a finish has been applied to the frame, the dowels will be glued in place. Apply glue in the dowel hole and tap the dowels into place. For now, set the dowels aside until after finishing.

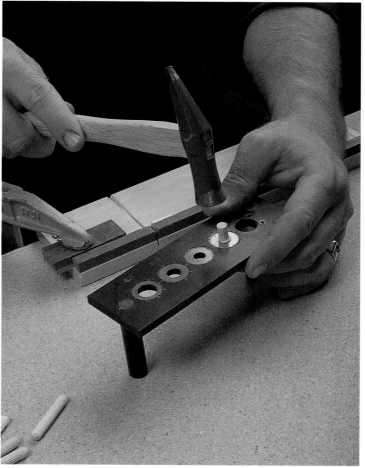

The careful work in making the top and frame square and accurate pays off at
this stage. If an edge banding fits too snuggly against one of the legs, it can be
carefully pared with a sharp chisel. A very fine paring cut on the end of an edge
banding may make a big difference in the fit of the top, so work carefully.

A number of finishes would be appropriate for a coffee table project. Some appropriate considerations would be varnish, lacquer, water-based urethane, varnish/oil combinations, and oil. I've chosen to use "Liberon Finishing Oil" for the tables shown in this book. The finishing oil brings out the rich tones in these woods and provides protection from water, heat, and alcohol, is easy to apply, and has soft sheen. It also does not require a dust free environment and dries very quickly.

I've placed small masking tape squares over the dowel holes so oil doesn't interfere with the glue joint. Starting with the base, pour a good amount of finishing oil on a rag and apply generously to the entire frame surface. As the oil soaks in, apply more. The tops of the legs will soak in quickly, so apply several applications. After 15 minutes wipe all remaining oil off the base, using a couple off dry rags. A dry, inexpensive brush will remove oil from difficult to reach areas. Once all excess oil has been removed, set the base aside to dry overnight.

Left: To finish the table top, pour some oil onto the top surface and spread a thick layer around the surface. It's always fun to see the rich colors of the wood come alive once the finish is applied.

Below left: Continue applying oil until the surface is covered. Also oil the edges of the table.

Below right: Apply additional oil as the initial coat soaks into the surface and the edges.

After about 15 minutes remove all excess oil with clean, dry rags. Within a few minutes some of the soaked in oil may "bleed" to the surface and need to be buffed off. Wipe off any bleeding before it cures or you'll have some extra work to do cutting the cured blisters of oil with sandpaper or steel wool. Check the surface every few minutes for bleeding, buffing off if necessary, then the top can be left to dry. After the surface has been buffed, turn the top over and oil the bottom side in the same manner. When the bottom side has been buffed dry it's a good time to check the top side for any bleeding and buff it away. Allow to dry overnight.

After the oil has dried, sand the surfaces with 400 grit sandpaper to smooth out the finish. Apply a second coat of oil to both the base and the top, repeating the process. Make sure to remove oil from hard to reach areas, as well as any bleeding that may occur. After drying overnight again, rub out the frame and top again with 0000 steel wool, working with the grain to cut the finish. Vacuum or blow off the steel wool particles. Apply a third coat of oil to the table top. A third coat on the base is a matter of personal judgment. This is not an area that is likely to be subject to spills, so I usually base the decision on how the sheen looks after two coats. I often apply three coats to the top, depending on the wood. Close grained woods like maple will require fewer coats than a more porous wood to acquire a satin sheen. Use steel wool after each finish coat and after the final coat to even out the sheen. Buff with a clean, soft cloth.

With the table nearly complete, I carve my initials on the bottom side of the table top. The top can now be glued to the base. Glue in the pre-cut dowels to the rails as previously described and tap in place. Apply glue in each of the dowel holes in the top panel and press the top into place on the base. I use padded cam clamps to gently squeeze the top tight to the base. Let the table set for a couple of hours. Remove the clamps and buff off any finger prints or marks.

Stand back and admire your work and be prepared for some coffee table orders from friends and family!

A FEW FAVORITES

Stickered 8/4 planks of narra and kwila from Papua, New Guinea. These ecologically harvested species are available from EcoTimber International, a company supplying woods from well managed forest operations.

A Japanese chamfer plane made of Japanese white oak with a high quality laminated blade. The special adjustable sole provides an automatic stop for a very smooth, even chamfer.

A hand forged laminated Japanese plane iron and breaker.

A special hand made Japanese chisel showing the double hollow ground area on the flat back. The hollow area, common to most Japanese chisels and irons, reduces the amount of flattening required when preparing the blade for use. This tool is made by Chutaro Imai, a highly skilled Japanese chisel maker.

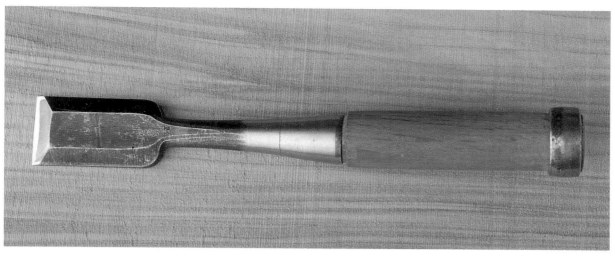

Above: A traditional Japanese chisel (Nomi). Many artisans prefer Japanese chisels over western chisels for the high quality of steel, as well as their fine balance and beauty.

Left: Japanese chisel showing the laminated steel blade. The harder steel creates a long lasting cutting edge, while the dense, softer steel absorbs impact and supports the cutting edge.

Above: Bronze scraper plane made by Lie-Nielsen is one of my favorite hand tools. This 5 1/2" plane is well suited for many applications and can be used with one or two hands. I highly recommend adding this tool to your collection.

Left: Bedrock jointer plane # 607. This antique was made prior to 1914, and represents the high end of quality for this type of metal bench plane. It's outfitted with an excellent blade made by Ron Hock.

GALLERY

154

GLOSSARY

Bench dog. A wooden or metal pin that fits into a hole or slot, called a bench dog hole, on a workbench to help keep a workpiece in place.

Bench puppies. Shop made fixtures that fit into the bench dog holes of a workbench for supporting a large panel vertically over the edge.

Board foot. A method of measuring lumber, describing a piece of wood 12" x 12" x 1"" thick. To determine the board footage of a plank, multiply the thickness times the width times the length in inches. Then divide the resulting number by 144 to arrive at the board feet.

Book-match. Two halves of a piece of wood or veneer that when opened like a book, create a mirror image of each other.

Bow. A lumber defect characterized by an end-to-end curve along the face of the board.

Brad-point bit. A drill bit with a sharp centerpoint and two cutting spurs. Brad-point bits produce cleaner holes than regular twist bits.

Cabinetmakers triangle. A triangular mark drawn on a board to aid in reassembling veneers in the sequence that they were cut.

Caul. A flat piece of wood used to distribute pressure evenly when clamping.

Chamfer. A corner or edge that is beveled to an angle, usually 45 degrees.

Chatoyance. Describes the reflective or iridescent quality in some woods.

Cheek. The wide surface or face of a tenon, perpendicular to the shoulder.

Commercial veneers. Very thin slices of wood, usually 1/28" or 1/40" thick.

Cup. A lumber defect characterized by edge-to-edge curve, resulting in a concave face.

Cut-off box. A wooden sled, fitted to a table saw top, used to support a workpiece while being cut.

Dowel center. A metal pin that is inserted into a dowel hole to locate a matching hole in an adjoining board.

Dozuki saw. A single sided Japanese saw used for cross-cutting.

Drift. The angle at which a bandsaw blade naturally cuts.

Dry run. A practice run of going completely through a glue-up procedure before applying glue.

Edge banding. Solid wood or veneer piece that is applied to the exposed edge of a plywood or MDF panel in a piece of furniture.

Edge gluing. Adhering boards or veneers together, edge-to-edge to create a panel or sheet.

End grain. The end of a piece of wood exposed by a cut across the grain.

End mill. A spiral fluted cutter, similar to a router bit, used in mortising.

Feather board. A piece of wood cut with tangs or "feathers" at one end, clamped in place to hold a workpiece against the fence of a saw or router table.

Fence. An adjustable guide used to keep a workpiece a set distance from a saw blade.

Figure. The pattern produced in a wood surface by the annual growth rings and color irregularities.

Grain. The arrangement of fibers in a piece of wood.

Grain graphic. The pattern or design presented by the arrangement of the grain of a piece of wood.

Grit. The number of grains of abrasive, per square inch, in sandpaper.

Guide blocks. Adjustable blocks of a friction resistant material that help prevent a bandsaw blade from flexing side-to-side.

Gullet. The fish hook, negative shape between the teeth of a saw blade.

Heartwood. The hard, nonliving wood at the core of a tree trunk. Usually darker than the sapwood.

Hollow grind. A hollow shape created on the bevel of a plane iron or chisel. The hollow grind reduces the surface of the bevel allowing for efficient sharpening.

Joinery. The art and science of joining wood pieces together.

Kerf. The width of material a saw blade takes out as it cuts.

Marking knife. A single-beveled knife used to mark a location on a workpiece.

Marquetry. A technique where different colors of wood veneers are cut to fit precisely together, creating a design in a single sheet.

MDF. Medium density fiberboard. A stable, man-made board often used as the core for a veneered panel.

Mock-up. A full-scale model made of common materials used to help visualize the proportions of a three-dimensional furniture piece.

Mortise. A rectangular or rounded hole cut into a piece of wood.

Mortise and tenon. A joinery technique in which a tenon on one board fits into the mortise of another board.

Nagura stone. A small, natural stone used to create a polishing slurry on the surface of fine Japanese water stones.

Plywood. A stable, man-made panel made of thin layers of wood glued tightly together.

Proud. An applied piece of wood that protrudes above or beyond an adjoining wood surface.

Push block. A devise used to safely push a workpiece into a moving blade or cutter to protect the hand.

Rail. A horizontal framework member of a table or other furniture piece.

Resawing. Sawing thin veneers out of solid wood planks.

Roed wood. Wood grain that grows in an interlocked fashion, making planing difficult. A ribbon-like grain pattern is common with roed wood.

Ryoba saw. A double-sided Japanese saw. One side is for ripping while the other is for cross-cuts.

Sapwood. The living wood from the outer part of a tree trunk. Often lighter in color than the heartwood.

Set. The slight offset of alternate teeth on a saw blade.

Shooting board. A wooden platform with an attached fence that allows the end of a workpiece to be trimmed or "shot" square with a hand plane.

Shoulder. In a mortise and tenon joint, the part of the tenon perpendicular to the cheek.

Snipe. A slightly deeper planer cut that occurs as a workpiece is being fed into and then exits a thickness planer.

Spline. A wood strip that fits into matching grooves of two pieces of wood being joined together.

Spline tenon. A variation of the traditional mortise-tenon joint, where a loose tenon joins a pair of mortises, such as in a rail-to-leg joint.

Squeeze out. Excess glue that is forced out of a glue joint when clamp pressure is applied.

Sticker. Thin strips of wood placed between planks or veneers to allow air flow around all surfaces.

Story stick. A length of wood used to transfer a measurement to a workpiece.

Tearout. The result of a blade or cutter that tears the wood fibers of the surface of a workpiece.

Tenon. The protrusion from the end of a board that fits into a mortise.

Veneer. A thin sheet of wood, usually no more than 1/8" thick.

Veneered panel. A panel with a thin layer of decorative wood applied to both sides.

Wood run. A trip in search of beautiful lumber. Always a joyous occasion.

SOURCE LIST

Eco Timber International
1020 Heinz Avenue
Berkeley, CA 94710
510-549-3000
Ecologically harvested domestic and imported lumber.

Hock Handmade Knives
16650 Mitchell Creek Drive
Fort Bragg, CA 95437
707-964-2782
High quality irons and blades for cutting tools.

Lie-Nielsen Toolworks
P.O. Box 9
Route 1
Warren, ME 04864
Bronze and steel hand planes.

The Japan Woodworker
1731 Clement Avenue
Alameda, CA 94702
Japanese woodworking tools.

Hida Tool and Hardware Company, Inc.
1333 San Pablo Avenue
Berkeley, CA 94702
510-524-3700
Japanese woodworking tools.